Editor

Erica N. Russikoff, M.A.

Contributing Editor

Michael H. Levin, M.A., N.B.C.T.

Cover Artist

Tony Carrillo

Editor in Chief

Ina Massler Levin, M.A.

Creative Director

Karen J. Goldfluss, M.S. Ed.

Imaging

Rosa C. See

Publisher

Mary D. Smith, M.S. Ed.

Prepare for Grade 6

Summertime Learning

Prepare Your Child for Sixth Grade

With 8 weeks worth of reading, writing, math and just plain fun!

includes over **300** stickers!

Teacher Created Resources

Teacher Created Resources

6421 Industry Way
Westminster, CA 92683
www.teachercreated.com

ISBN: 978-1-4206-8846-7

©2011 Teacher Created Resources
Reprinted, 2012 (PO5615)

Made in U.S.A.

Teacher Created Resources

Table of Contents

Table of Contents *(cont.)*

A Message From the
National Summer Learning Association

Dear Parents,

Did you know that all young people experience learning losses when they don't engage in educational activities during the summer? That means some of what they've spent time learning over the preceding school year evaporates during the summer months. However, summer learning loss is something that you can help prevent. Summer is the perfect time for fun and engaging activities that can help children maintain and grow their academic skills. Here are just a few:

- Encourage your child to read every day and to visit the local library frequently to select new books.

- Ask your child's teacher for recommendations of books for summer reading. The Summer Reading List in this publication is a good start.

- Explore parks, nature preserves, museums, and cultural centers.

- Consider every day as a day full of teachable moments. Measuring in recipes and reviewing maps before a car trip are ways to learn or reinforce a skill. Use the Learning Experiences in the back of this book for more ideas.

- Each day, set goals to accomplish. For example, do five math problems or read a chapter in a book.

- Encourage your child to complete the activities in books, such as *Summertime Learning*, to help bridge the summer learning gap.

Our vision is for every child to be safe, healthy, and engaged in learning during the summer. Learn more at *www.summerlearning.org* and *www.summerlearningcampaign.org*.

Have a *memorable* summer!

Brenda McLaughlin
Vice President, Strategic Initiatives
National Summer Learning Association

How to Use This Book

As a parent, you know that summertime is a time for fun and learning. So it is quite handy that fun and learning can go hand in hand when your child uses *Summertime Learning*.

There are many ways to use this book effectively with your child. We list three ideas on page 6. (See "Day by Day," "Pick and Choose," and "All of a Kind.") You may choose one way on one day, and, on another day, choose something else.

Book Organization

Summertime Learning is organized around an eight-week summer vacation period. For each weekday, there are two lessons. Each Monday through Thursday, there is a math lesson. Additionally, during the odd-numbered weeks, there is a reading lesson on Monday and Wednesday and a writing lesson on Tuesday and Thursday. During the even-numbered weeks, these lessons switch days. (Reading lessons are on Tuesday and Thursday, and writing lessons are on Monday and Wednesday.) Fridays feature two Friday Fun activities (one typically being a puzzle). The calendar looks like this:

Day	Week 1	Week 2	Week 3	Week 4	Week 5	Week 6	Week 7	Week 8
M	Math	Math	Math	Math	Math	Math	Math	Math
	Reading	Writing	Reading	Writing	Reading	Writing	Reading	Writing
T	Math	Math	Math	Math	Math	Math	Math	Math
	Writing	Reading	Writing	Reading	Writing	Reading	Writing	Reading
W	Math	Math	Math	Math	Math	Math	Math	Math
	Reading	Writing	Reading	Writing	Reading	Writing	Reading	Writing
Th	Math	Math	Math	Math	Math	Math	Math	Math
	Writing	Reading	Writing	Reading	Writing	Reading	Writing	Reading
F	Friday Fun	Friday Fun	Friday Fun	Friday Fun	Friday Fun	Friday Fun	Friday Fun	Friday Fun
	Friday Fun	Friday Fun	Friday Fun	Friday Fun	Friday Fun	Friday Fun	Friday Fun	Friday Fun

How to Use This Book

(cont.)

Day by Day

You can have your child do the activities in order, beginning on the first Monday of summer vacation. He or she can complete the two lessons provided for each day. It does not matter if math, reading, or writing is completed first. The pages are designed so that each day of the week's lessons are back to back. The book is also perforated. This gives you the option of tearing the pages out for your child to work on. If you opt to have your child tear out the pages, you might want to store the completed pages in a special folder or three-ring binder that your child decorates.

Pick and Choose

You may find that you do not want to have your child work strictly in order. Feel free to pick and choose any combination of pages based on your child's needs and interests.

All of a Kind

Perhaps your child needs more help in one area than another. You may opt to have him or her work only on math, reading, or writing.

Keeping Track

A Reward Chart is included on page 10 of this book, so you and your child can keep track of the activities that have been completed. This page is designed to be used with the stickers provided. Once your child has finished a page, have him or her put a sticker on the castle. If you don't want to use stickers for this, have your child color in a circle each time an activity is completed.

The stickers can also be used on the individual pages. As your child finishes a page, let him or her place a sticker in the sun at the top of the page. If he or she asks where to begin the next day, simply have him or her start on the page after the last sticker.

There are enough stickers to use for both the Reward Chart and the sun on each page. Plus, there are extra stickers for children to enjoy.

Standards and Skills

Each activity in *Summertime Learning* meets one or more of the following strategies and skills*. The activities in this book are designed to help your child reinforce the skills learned during fifth grade, as well as introduce new skills that will be learned in sixth grade.

Language Arts Standards

- ✿ Uses the general skills and strategies of the writing process
- ✿ Uses the stylistic and rhetorical aspects of writing
- ✿ Uses grammatical and mechanical conventions in written composition
- ✿ Gathers and uses information for research purposes
- ✿ Uses the general skills and strategies of the reading process
- ✿ Uses skills and strategies to read a variety of literary texts
- ✿ Uses skills and strategies to read a variety of informational texts

Mathematics Standards

- ✿ Uses a variety of strategies in the problem-solving process
- ✿ Understands and applies basic and advanced properties of the concepts of numbers
- ✿ Uses basic and advanced procedures while performing the processes of computation
- ✿ Understands and applies basic and advanced properties of the concepts of measurement
- ✿ Understands and applies basic and advanced properties of the concepts of geometry
- ✿ Understands and applies basic and advanced concepts of statistics and data analysis
- ✿ Understands and applies basic and advanced concepts of probability
- ✿ Understands and applies basic and advanced properties of functions and algebra

Writing Skills

- ✿ Uses a variety of strategies to draft and revise written work
- ✿ Uses a variety of strategies to edit and publish written work
- ✿ Evaluates own and others' writing
- ✿ Uses style, content, and structure appropriate for specific audiences and purposes
- ✿ Writes expository compositions
- ✿ Writes in response to literature
- ✿ Uses descriptive language that clarifies and enhances ideas
- ✿ Uses paragraph form in writing
- ✿ Uses a variety of sentence structures to expand and imbed ideas
- ✿ Uses pronouns in written compositions
- ✿ Uses nouns in written compositions
- ✿ Uses verbs in written compositions
- ✿ Uses adjectives in written compositions
- ✿ Uses adverbs in written compositions

Standards and Skills
(cont.)

Writing Skills *(cont.)*

✿ Uses prepositions and coordinating conjunctions in written compositions

✿ Uses conventions of spelling in written compositions

✿ Uses conventions of capitalization in written compositions

✿ Uses conventions of punctuation in written compositions

Reading Skills

✿ Establishes and adjusts purposes for reading

✿ Uses a variety of strategies to extend reading vocabulary

✿ Understands level-appropriate reading vocabulary

✿ Reads a variety of literary passages and texts

✿ Knows the defining features and structural elements of a variety of literary genres

✿ Understands complex elements of plot development

✿ Understands elements of character development

✿ Understands the use of specific literary devices

✿ Understands point of view in a literary text

✿ Makes connections between characters or the causes for complex events in texts and those in his or her own life

✿ Reads a variety of informational texts

✿ Knows the defining structural characteristics and features used in informational texts

✿ Summarizes and paraphrases information in texts

✿ Uses new information to adjust and extend personal knowledge base

✿ Draws conclusions and makes inferences based on explicit and implicit information in texts

Mathematics Skills

✿ Understands how to break a complex problem into simpler parts or use a similar problem type to solve a problem

✿ Uses a variety of strategies to understand problem-solving situations and processes

✿ Understands that there is no one right way to solve mathematical problems but that different methods have different advantages and disadvantages

✿ Formulates a problem, determines information required to solve the problem, chooses methods for obtaining this information, and sets limits for acceptable solutions

✿ Understands the role of written symbols in representing mathematical ideas and the use of precise language in conjunction with the special symbols of mathematics

✿ Understands the relationships among equivalent number representations and the advantages and disadvantages of each type of representation

Mathematics Skills *(cont.)*

- ✿ Understands the characteristics and properties of the set of rational numbers and its subsets
- ✿ Understands the role of positive and negative integers in the number system
- ✿ Uses number theory concepts to solve problems
- ✿ Understands the characteristics and uses of exponents and scientific notation
- ✿ Understands the concepts of ratio, proportion, and percent and the relationships among them
- ✿ Adds, subtracts, multiplies, and divides integers and rational numbers
- ✿ Adds and subtracts fractions with unlike denominators; multiplies and divides fractions
- ✿ Understands the correct order of operations for performing arithmetic computations
- ✿ Uses proportional reasoning to solve mathematical and real-world problems
- ✿ Understands the properties of operations with rational numbers
- ✿ Understands the basic concept of rate as a measure
- ✿ Solves problems involving perimeter (circumference) and area of various shapes
- ✿ Understands the relationships among linear dimensions, area, and volume and the corresponding uses of units, square units, and cubic units of measure
- ✿ Solves problems involving units of measurement and converts answers to a larger or smaller unit within the same system
- ✿ Understands formulas for finding measures
- ✿ Understands the defining properties of three-dimensional figures
- ✿ Understands the defining properties of triangles
- ✿ Understands basic characteristics of measures of central tendency
- ✿ Reads and interprets data in charts, tables, and plots
- ✿ Uses data and statistical measures for a variety of purposes
- ✿ Understands faulty arguments, common errors, and misleading presentations of data
- ✿ Determines probability using mathematical/theoretical models
- ✿ Understands how predictions are based on data and probabilities
- ✿ Understands various representations of patterns and functions and the relationships among them
- ✿ Solves linear equations using concrete, informal, and formal methods
- ✿ Understands basic operations on algebraic expressions

* Standards and skills used with permission from McREL (Copyright 2011, McREL. Midcontinent Research for Education and Learning. Address: 4601 DTC Boulevard, Suite 500, Denver, CO 80237. Telephone: 303-337-0990. Web site: *www.mcrel.org/standards-benchmarks*). To align McREL Standards to the Common Core Standards, go to *www.mcrel.org*.

Reward Chart

Add Three Numbers

Directions: Solve each problem. Write each sum in the number puzzle.

Across

2.
$$\begin{array}{r} 713 \\ 595 \\ + 664 \\ \hline \end{array}$$

3.
$$\begin{array}{r} 184 \\ 432 \\ + 629 \\ \hline \end{array}$$

4.
$$\begin{array}{r} 711 \\ 490 \\ + 528 \\ \hline \end{array}$$

5.
$$\begin{array}{r} 572 \\ 444 \\ + 783 \\ \hline \end{array}$$

6.
$$\begin{array}{r} 881 \\ 357 \\ + 795 \\ \hline \end{array}$$

7.
$$\begin{array}{r} 751 \\ 953 \\ + 642 \\ \hline \end{array}$$

8.
$$\begin{array}{r} 487 \\ 507 \\ + 109 \\ \hline \end{array}$$

10.
$$\begin{array}{r} 512 \\ 579 \\ + 830 \\ \hline \end{array}$$

11.
$$\begin{array}{r} 314 \\ 973 \\ + 818 \\ \hline \end{array}$$

12.
$$\begin{array}{r} 838 \\ 564 \\ + 266 \\ \hline \end{array}$$

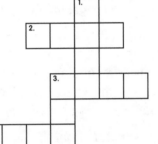

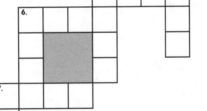

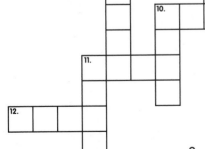

Down

1.
$$\begin{array}{r} 134 \\ 958 \\ + 620 \\ \hline \end{array}$$

3.
$$\begin{array}{r} 469 \\ 581 \\ + 141 \\ \hline \end{array}$$

4.
$$\begin{array}{r} 411 \\ 925 \\ + 634 \\ \hline \end{array}$$

5.
$$\begin{array}{r} 801 \\ 345 \\ + 162 \\ \hline \end{array}$$

6.
$$\begin{array}{r} 771 \\ 825 \\ + 877 \\ \hline \end{array}$$

7.
$$\begin{array}{r} 729 \\ 629 \\ + 746 \\ \hline \end{array}$$

8.
$$\begin{array}{r} 310 \\ 266 \\ + 466 \\ \hline \end{array}$$

9.
$$\begin{array}{r} 643 \\ 583 \\ + 185 \\ \hline \end{array}$$

10.
$$\begin{array}{r} 451 \\ 999 \\ + 308 \\ \hline \end{array}$$

11.
$$\begin{array}{r} 861 \\ 849 \\ + 973 \\ \hline \end{array}$$

The Aztecs

Directions: Read the passage, and then circle the correct answers below.

The Aztecs were the last people to settle in the Valley of Mexico, high in the volcanic mountains of central Mexico. There, on the shores of shallow, marshy Lake Tezcoco, they built an impressive center for their empire.

The Aztecs were a semi-nomadic tribe of Chichimecs who arrived in the Valley of Mexico about 1200 CE. According to oral traditions and codices (ancient manuscripts), the ancestral home of the Aztecs was Aztlan, a place northwest of Mexico City. No one has identified an exact location. Legend has it that about 1100 CE, the god Huizilopochtli (Blue Hummingbird) instructed them to wander until they found an eagle on a cactus eating a snake. There they would build their capital.

After many stops and skirmishes, they settled on the west side of Tezcoco, at a place called Chapultapec (Grasshopper Hill). Other tribes drove the Aztecs out, but the Colhua allowed the Aztecs to live near them in exchange for the services of Aztec soldiers. Finally tired of being under the Colhuacans, the Aztecs killed the daughter of the ruler and then fled into the marshy lake. On one island, they saw an eagle on a cactus. At the site of this sign, the Aztecs built their capital, Tenochtitlán.

In the 200 years from the sighting of the eagle (about 1325 CE) to the arrival of the Spanish (1521 CE), the Aztecs grew to be the most powerful people in the Valley of Mexico. They adopted many elements from the cultures that had preceded them and built one of the most impressive cities of Mesoamerica.

1. Based on the passage, how do you think people first learned about the Aztecs?

   a. reading textbooks

   b. oral traditions and codices

   c. in the newspaper

   d. on the Internet

2. What does *Huizilopochtli* mean?

   a. Valley of Mexico

   b. Blue Hummingbird

   c. Grasshopper Hill

   d. capital city

3. The Aztec capital was named

   a. Aztlan.

   b. Tezcoco.

   c. Tenochtitlán.

   d. Mesoamerica.

4. What sign did the Aztecs look for to know where to build their capital?

   a. an eagle on a cactus

   b. a fish in the lake

   c. lightning hitting the mountain

   d. a blue hummingbird

Multiply Supplies

Directions: Use the chart to solve each problem below. The first one has been done for you.

Supply Room Inventory

pencils	**erasers**	**crayons**	**markers**
68 per box	847 per box	271 per box	199 per box
rulers	**notepads**	**hole punchers**	**binders**
952 per box	88 per box	348 per box	17 per box
pens	**rubber bands**	**sheets of paper**	**folders**
1,107 per box	23 per box	7,127 per box	1,104 per box

1. 61 boxes of rulers $\begin{array}{r} 952 \\ \times\ \ 61 \\ \hline 952 \\ +\ 57,120 \\ \hline 58,072 \end{array}$	2. 37 boxes of pencils	3. 58 boxes of binders	4. 759 boxes of erasers
5. 373 boxes of notepads	6. 19 boxes of pens	7. 99 boxes of rubber bands	8. 314 boxes of hole punchers
9. 510 boxes of paper	10. 217 boxes of markers	11. 71 boxes of crayons	12. 861 boxes of folders

Sensory Words

Sensory words are words that describe how something *feels, looks, sounds, smells,* or *tastes.*

Directions: Write a sentence that uses one of the five senses to describe each of the following. Circle the word that describes how the item feels, looks, sounds, smells, or tastes. On the line after the sentence, write which of the senses you used. The first one has been done for you.

1. soccer ball   I wiped off the (dusty) soccer ball.   looks

2. pizza

3. camel

4. sports announcer

5. notebook

6. tennis shoes

7. desert

8. beach

9. surprise

10. happiness

11. embarrassment

12. snake

13. rock

14. lemon

Divide and Multiply

Directions: Write the division problem and solve. Multiply to check the answer. The first one has been done for you.

1. 8,400 cookies divided into 40 boxes	2. 41,916 pieces of bubble gum divided into 28 cartons	3. 33,320 decks of playing cards divided into 136 cases
Solve **Check**	**Solve** **Check**	**Solve** **Check**

For problem 1:

Solve

$$40\overline{)8400}$$ quotient 210

-80

$\ \ 40$

-40

$\ \ 000$

Check

210

$\times\ \ 40$

000

$+\ 8,400$

$8,400$

4. 3,600 marbles placed into 90 pouches	5. 8,928 potato chips placed into 9 gigantic bowls	6. 28,917 game pieces for 81 board games
Solve **Check**	**Solve** **Check**	**Solve** **Check**

7. 35,620 paper clips placed into 260 canisters	8. 180,930 ants in 37 colonies	9. 8,840 peanuts for 65 elephants
Solve **Check**	**Solve** **Check**	**Solve** **Check**

Mexico: Past and Present

Directions: Read the passage, and then circle the correct answers below.

Hundreds of years ago, American Indian tribes lived in Mexico. The Aztecs built beautiful cities. They had a calendar and a written language. However, the Spanish destroyed the Aztecs in 1521. For the next 300 years, Spain ruled over Mexico. That's why Mexicans speak Spanish.

Every September 16, the Mexican people hold a celebration in Mexico City, their country's capital. It is their Independence Day. On that date in 1821, they told Spain they would no longer be ruled. Breaking free from Spain caused a war. When it was over, the Mexicans had their own government. They made their own laws.

Today, America and Mexico are friends, but it wasn't always that way. President James Polk wanted America to reach from the Atlantic Ocean to the Pacific Ocean. He tried to buy what is now the American Southwest from Mexico. Mexico would not sell. So from 1846 to 1848, Mexico and America fought a war to **ascertain** where their borders would be. When the war ended, Mexico had lost a lot of land. Now the Rio Grande River forms the border between the two nations. America is on the north side of the river. Mexico is on the south side.

Mexico has mountains and a hot, dry climate. Crops can grow on only a small part of the land. Still, Mexicans grow much of the coffee, oranges, and sugar used in the United States. Mexicans have influenced building styles in the southwestern U.S. and have added words such as *patio* and *canyon* to the English language. Americans also enjoy eating many Mexican foods like burritos, tacos, tortillas, and tamales.

1. President Polk wanted
   a. the U.S. to expand its borders.
   b. Mexico to change its Independence Day to July 4th.
   c. the country of Mexico to become one of the states of the Union.
   d. Americans to adopt the Mexican language.

2. According to the passage, what happened second?
   a. Mexicans declared their independence from Spain.
   b. The Spanish ruled over Mexico.
   c. The Aztecs built cities in Mexico.
   d. Americans fought a war with Mexico.

3. Another word for *ascertain* is
   a. inspect.   b. change.   c. discover.   d. determine.

4. Before the Aztecs were conquered, they probably
   a. didn't speak Spanish.   c. didn't have any tools.
   b. couldn't read or write any language.   d. didn't understand the concept of time.

Multiplying Decimals

Directions: Multiply to solve each problem.

Keys to Multiplying Decimals

✿ Line up the numbers. However, you don't need to line up the decimal points.

✿ Multiply the numbers as you would multiply whole numbers.

✿ Count the number of decimal places in both numbers that are being multiplied. Make sure the decimal places in the product equal the number of decimal places in the problem.

1.
$$\begin{array}{r} \$46.98 \\ \times \quad 2 \\ \hline \end{array}$$

2.
$$\begin{array}{r} \$1.49 \\ \times \quad 3 \\ \hline \end{array}$$

3.
$$\begin{array}{r} \$21.06 \\ \times \quad 5 \\ \hline \end{array}$$

4.
$$\begin{array}{r} \$9.99 \\ \times \quad 7 \\ \hline \end{array}$$

5.
$$\begin{array}{r} \$1.57 \\ \times \quad 34 \\ \hline \end{array}$$

6.
$$\begin{array}{r} \$105.13 \\ \times \quad 4 \\ \hline \end{array}$$

7.
$$\begin{array}{r} \$45.03 \\ \times \quad 13 \\ \hline \end{array}$$

8.
$$\begin{array}{r} \$17.10 \\ \times \quad 15 \\ \hline \end{array}$$

9.
$$\begin{array}{r} 0.84 \\ \times \quad 3.15 \\ \hline \end{array}$$

10.
$$\begin{array}{r} 2.08 \\ \times \quad 0.9 \\ \hline \end{array}$$

11.
$$\begin{array}{r} 0.28 \\ \times \quad 9.51 \\ \hline \end{array}$$

12.
$$\begin{array}{r} 0.0076 \\ \times \quad 0.30 \\ \hline \end{array}$$

13.
$$\begin{array}{r} \$10.50 \\ \times \quad 0.60 \\ \hline \end{array}$$

14.
$$\begin{array}{r} 47.8 \\ \times \quad 0.1 \\ \hline \end{array}$$

15.
$$\begin{array}{r} 14.2 \\ \times \quad 9.7 \\ \hline \end{array}$$

16.
$$\begin{array}{r} \$5.75 \\ \times \quad 0.24 \\ \hline \end{array}$$

17.
$$\begin{array}{r} \$5.58 \\ \times \quad 1.5 \\ \hline \end{array}$$

18.
$$\begin{array}{r} 0.14 \\ \times \quad 0.87 \\ \hline \end{array}$$

Connections

Directions: Think of a word that could be used with each given word to make a compound word or phrase. The first one has been done for you.

1. opera	box	hand	_____soap_____
2. head	Easter	fried	_____
3. Christmas	flies	Magazine	_____
4. whipped	sour	cheese	_____
5. shelter	atomic	time	_____
6. book	garbage	pipe	_____
7. light	cards	back	_____
8. go	wheel	shopping	_____
9. moon	night	year	_____
10. city	way	mark	_____
11. Adam's	tree	core	_____
12. ballpoint	pal	pig	_____
13. power	shoe	race	_____
14. birds	sick	puppy	_____
15. ball	lid	pink	_____

Map Madness!

Do you see Juanita? She is lost! Follow the directions to get her back on track. Mark her ending spot with an **X**.

Directions:

1.   Go north on 2nd Ave.

2. ➡ Turn right on Union St.

3. ➡ Turn right on 4th Ave.

4. ⬅ Turn left on Spring St.

5. ➡ Turn right on 5th Ave.

6. **END** End at the corner of James St.

7th Ave.

Union St.

6th Ave.

Seneca St.

3rd Ave.

Spring St.

4th Ave.

2nd Ave.

Olivia St.

8th Ave.

1st Ave.

Marion St.

5th Ave.

James St.

Hidden Animals

Directions: The name of one animal is hidden in each sentence. It is not one of the obvious animal names used and may be hidden inside one or several words. Can you find each one? Circle each name and write it on the line. The first one has been done for you.

1. Jim (was) painting a picture.

   _____ wasp _____

2. The car I bought yesterday is shiny and beautiful.

   _____

3. Mary took a picture of a panther in a cage.

   _____

4. All amazing tricks are fascinating.

   _____

5. Ramon keys into more projects than other kids.

   _____

6. My new neighbor, Mo, uses peppers on his pizza.

   _____

7. To and fro, Gary pushed his sister on the swing.

   _____

8. Jennifer ate three pieces of fudge.

   _____

9. The team of oxen pulled the wagon.

   _____

10. The new car glimmered in the light.

    _____

Temperature Puzzle

Math

Directions: Use the formulas in the box below to convert each temperature. Write each temperature to the hundredths place without rounding and complete the number puzzle. Be sure to include the decimal points in the puzzle. Clue #1 Across has been done for you.

Formulas

°F to °C: subtract 32°, then divide by 1.8

°C to °F: multiply by 1.8, then add 32°

Across

1. 40°F = __4.44__ °C
2. 77°F = _____ °C
3. 45°F = _____ °C
5. 35°F = _____ °C
6. 91°F = _____ °C
7. 61°F = _____ °C
8. 76°C = _____ °F
12. 25°C = _____ °F
14. 36°C = _____ °F
15. 7°C = _____ °F
17. 93°C = _____ °F
18. 68°F = _____ °C

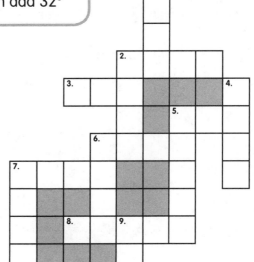

Down

1. 114°F = _____ °C
2. 72°F = _____ °C
4. 80°F = _____ °C
5. 82°C = _____ °F
6. 89°F = _____ °C
7. 56°F = _____ °C
9. 30°C = _____ °F
10. 3°C = _____ °F
11. 47°C = _____ °F
13. 90°C = _____ °F
16. 32°C = _____ °F
17. 51°C = _____ °F

Antonym Crossword

Directions: Fill in the crossword puzzle with the antonyms of the words below. *Hint:* Most of the answers start with "C" or "D." Clue #8 Across has been done for you.

Across

The antonym of . . .

3.	rare	11.	contrast
4.	pick up	12.	alive
8.	avoid	13.	open
9.	destroy	14.	hot
10.	cheerful	17.	laughed

Down

The antonym of . . .

1.	go	11.	straight
2.	incorrect	12.	shallow
3.	original	13.	sane
5.	cloudless	15.	night
6.	uncovered	16.	light
7.	unimportant		

Changing Time

Part I

Directions: Complete the chart by converting hours into minutes and seconds.

	Hours	Minutes	Seconds
1.	$\frac{1}{4}$		
2.	$\frac{1}{2}$		
3.	$\frac{3}{4}$		
4.	1		
5.	2		
6.	3		
7.	4		
8.	6		
9.	8		
10.	12		
11.	18		
12.	24		

Part II

Directions: Use the **<** or **>** symbols to compare each pair of times.

1.
210 seconds $\bigcirc$ 2 minutes

2.
98 minutes $\bigcirc$ 5 hours

3.
27 minutes $\bigcirc$ 630 seconds

4.
4 hours $\bigcirc$ 6,641 seconds

Mummies in Ancient Egypt

Directions: Read the passage, and then circle the correct answers.

Thousands of years ago, people in Ancient Egypt thought that dead people needed their bodies after death. They believed that the people continued to live in a place called the afterlife, so they found a way to keep dead bodies from rotting. They figured out how to turn dead people into mummies. They **preserved** most of their kings and queens this way.

It was a lot of work to make a mummy. First, priests washed the dead body. Then they removed all of the organs—even the brain! They put a kind of salt all over the body. After six weeks, the body completely dried out. Next, they stuffed the body with sand, sawdust, or cloth. This made the body look full again. Then they rubbed spices and oils into the skin. Finally, the priests wrapped cloth strips tightly around each part of the body. Wrapping the body took about two weeks. Lastly, they put the body into a coffin. On its cover, the coffin had paintings and sometimes gems.

The most famous mummy is King Tut. He was still a teenager when he died over 4,000 years ago. He was put into a secret tomb. Scientists found this tomb in 1922. His family had put all sorts of gold, gems, and other riches into his tomb. Inside, King Tut's mummy lay in a solid gold coffin. Even his sandals were made of solid gold.

1. Ancient Egyptians believed dead kings and queens

    a. would use their belongings after they died.

    b. should be burned instead of buried.

    c. would send good luck to their people.

    d. would return to their throne after they died.

2. What did the priests do last when making a mummy?

    a. They washed the body.   c. They wrapped the body.

    b. They removed the organs.   d. They stuffed the body.

3. Egyptians mummified their rulers because

    a. they thought it would make the rulers look better in the afterlife.

    b. they thought the rulers needed their bodies in the afterlife.

    c. they wanted to use the rulers' organs.

    d. they hoped the rulers would be found years later.

4. The opposite of *preserved* is

    a. kept.   c. ruined.

    b. worshipped.   d. changed.

Multiplying Decimals II

Math

Directions: Solve each multiplication problem. Write each product in the number puzzle. Be sure to include the decimal points in the puzzle. Clue #2 Across has been done for you.

Across

2. 9.726 x 3 = __29.178__

4. 3.82 x 2 = _____

6. 4.2 x 7 = _____

7. 7.3 x 3 = _____

9. 9.8 x 5 = _____

10. .12 x 7 = _____

12. 7.5 x 8 = _____

13. .69 x 6 = _____

14. 8.008 x 7 = _____

17. 8.386 x 4 = _____

Down

1. .47 x 4 = _____

2. 1.3201 x 2 = _____

3. 5.80 x 3 = _____

5. 2.11 x 4 = _____

6. 7.068 x 3 = _____

8. 6.4 x 2 = _____

11. 9.21 x 5 = _____

13. .54 x 9 = _____

15. 5.95 x 9 = _____

16. .17 x 2 = _____

How Many Uses?

Many words from daily conversation and writing can be used in a variety of ways. One example is the word *quarter*:

☼ Avery saves all his *quarters* in his largest piggy bank. (noun)

☼ A *quarter* portion of the estate was given to each of the four heirs. (adjective)

☼ *Quarter* the apple pie so that we can all have a piece. (verb)

Directions: Use each of these words two different ways. Use a dictionary to check the words' various definitions.

1. fast

   a. _____

   b. _____

2. side

   a. _____

   b. _____

3. number

   a. _____

   b. _____

4. good

   a. _____

   b. _____

5. just

   a. _____

   b. _____

6. retreat

   a. _____

   b. _____

Car Calculations

Directions: Use your knowledge of decimal operations to compare the results for each car tested.

1. A station wagon traveled 248.9 miles on a tank of gas. A sedan traveled 218.576 miles on a tank of gas. How far did they travel altogether? _____

2. A hybrid car is powered by a combination of electrical batteries and gasoline. This vehicle traveled 112.34 miles on one gallon of gasoline. How many miles would it travel on 20 gallons of gasoline? _____

3. The stopping distance for the Laser Racer was 45.678 feet. The stopping distance for the Super Sport was 78.1 feet. What is the difference? _____

4. A regular gasoline-powered car traveled exactly 18.2 miles on a gallon of gasoline. The hybrid car went 112.34 miles on a gallon of gas. How much farther did the hybrid car travel on one gallon? _____

5. The New Wave Motor Company has developed an SUV which travels 380.75 miles on 25 gallons of gasoline. How far can it travel on 1 gallon of gasoline? _____

6. A sports car traveled 198.764 miles on one tank of gas. A sedan traveled 243.4 miles on one tank of gas. How much farther did the sedan travel? _____

7. The maximum speed of a battery-powered vehicle was 42.387 miles per hour. The maximum speed of a gasoline-powered roadster was 220.2 miles per hour. How much faster was the roadster? _____

8. A classic car from the 1960s weighs 4,173.96 pounds. A battery-powered experimental vehicle weighs 1,143.003 pounds. How much heavier is the classic car? _____

9. An experimental car traveled 819.45 miles on 9 gallons of gas. How far did it travel on 1 gallon of gas? _____

10. An experimental motorcycle can travel 189.34 miles on a gallon of gas. How far could it travel on a full tank holding 4.65 gallons of gas? _____

The Underground Army

Directions: Read the passage, and then circle the correct answers.

Qin Shi Huangdi was a great Chinese emperor. He was the first emperor of the Qin dynasty. A dynasty is a series of rulers from the same family. The Qin dynasty began over 2,200 years ago when Qin unified several small states. Qin unified the states under a strong central government.

Qin is famous for a wall. The wall is known as the Great Wall of China. The Great Wall of China is over 2,000 miles long. Qin built it to protect the country against intruders. An intruder is one who forces himself or herself upon others. The Great Wall is high and wide. Astronauts can pick it out as they orbit Earth because of its size.

Qin is also famous for an army. The army is made up of over 7,500 warriors. Some of the warriors stand at attention. Other warriors, such as the archers, kneel. These warriors are armed with spears, bows, and arrows. Other armed warriors are on horses. Qin's army can still be seen today. One can understand how Qin's wall can still be seen today, but how is it possible to view Qin's army?

In 1974, two farmers were digging a well in central China. When their hole was about 14 feet deep, their shovels hit something hard. They thought it was a terra-cotta pot. Terra-cotta pots are dull brownish-red. They are made of clay. As the farmers dug further, they were shocked at what they found. Instead of a pot, they found a head! They were even more astounded when they found the head was attached to a body!

Archaeologists were called in. Archaeologists study ancient times and ancient peoples. The archaeologists were astounded at the find. The terra-cotta warrior was life-size. His face was perfectly sculpted, or formed. As the archaeologists continued to dig, they found an entire life-size army standing in formation 20 feet below the ground. Each warrior had a perfectly sculpted head, no two of which were the same. Each warrior had real weapons. Qin built the terra-cotta army to protect his tomb!

1. This story is mainly about
   a. what Qin did.
   b. ancient China.
   c. the Great Wall.
   d. what archaeologists found.

2. Qin's army is made up of over
   a. 20 warriors.
   b. 2,200 warriors.
   c. 7,500 warriors.
   d. 75,200 warriors.

3. One can view Qin's army today because
   a. it is life-size.
   b. it has been uncovered.
   c. it is made of terra cotta.
   d. it was built to protect Qin's tomb.

4. Think about how the word *intruder* relates to *guest*. What words relate in the same way?
   a. ancient : old
   b. terra cotta : clay
   c. unified : separate
   d. surprised : astounded

After-School Hours

Directions: Read each clue. If the answer is "yes," make an **O** in the box. If the answer is "no," make an **X** in the box.

Clues

☼ Ana went to her event earlier in the week than Steve.

☼ Maria went to the sporting event but not on Monday.

☼ Dave went to the premiere of *Attack of the Bugs* on Tuesday.

☼ Steve went to the new art exhibit on Wednesday.

	Monday	Tuesday	Wednesday	Thursday	Art Exhibit	Fair	Movie Premiere	Sporting Event
Ana								
Dave								
Maria								
Steve								

1. Ana went to the _____ on _____ .

2. Dave went to the _____ on _____ .

3. Maria went to the _____ on _____ .

4. Steve went to the _____ on _____ .

Sports Stumpers

Directions: Find the name of the football, basketball, baseball, or hockey team that fits each clue. Choose your answer from the Team List.

Team List

Braves	Jazz	Mets
Clippers	Kings	Nets
Colts	Lions	Padres
Eagles	Marlins	Pistons

1. tools used to help fishermen _____

2. fathers _____

3. multiple New York art museums _____

4. young horses _____

5. endangered birds _____

6. kings of the jungle _____

7. parts of a car _____

8. big fish _____

9. style of music _____

10. queens' spouses _____

11. scissors _____

12. bold and courageous _____

Exponents

Math

Directions: Calculate the answer to each problem. Write each answer in the number puzzle. Remember, the exponent tells the number of times to multiply the base by itself. Clue #2 Across has been done for you.

Across

2. 7^5 = <u>7 x 7 x 7 x 7 x 7 = 16,807</u>

3. 5^3 = _____

5. 11^3 = _____

10. 9^6 = _____

12. 7^2 = _____

13. 4^4 = _____

14. 5^4 = _____

16. 12^2 = _____

17. 11^4 = _____

19. 2^4 = _____

Reminder
exponent

$$7^5 ↵$$

base

Down

1. 10^3 = _____

2. 5^6 = _____

4. 3^5 = _____

6. 7^3 = _____

7. 8^4 = _____

8. 5^5 = _____

9. 9^4 = _____

11. 4^5 = _____

15. 8^3 = _____

18. 11^2 = _____

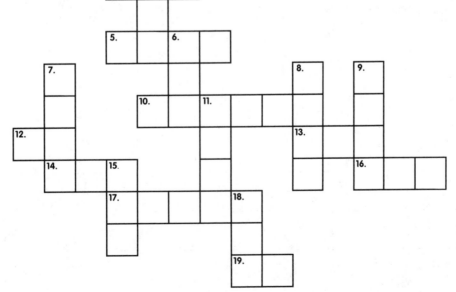

Main Ideas and Details

You can picture the main idea as a flag flying at the top of a pole. The flag is what you notice first. It's what's most important, just like the main idea. The flagpole holds up the flag, just as the details hold up, or support, the main idea. Details provide more facts about the main idea by offering reasons and giving examples.

Directions: Read the passage, and then circle the correct main idea. Write the supporting details from the passage on the lines.

> The explorers held their flashlights high as they cautiously moved forward. No sooner had they stepped inside the tunnel than a great monster leaped from the shadows and blocked their way. The ugly beast had purple eyes. Above them, a horn rose from the center of its forehead. Its bright orange skin showed beneath a thin layer of coarse, black hair. As it reached its claws toward the terrified group, it snarled menacingly, revealing a mouthful of sharp teeth.

The main idea is:

a. The explorers discover a secret tunnel.

b. A frightening monster stands before the explorers.

c. An evil monster threatens to eat the explorers.

d. The frightened explorers need to use flashlights inside a dark tunnel.

The main idea is supported by these six details:

1. _____

2. _____

3. _____

4. _____

5. _____

6. _____

Adding and Subtracting Integers

Directions: Solve each problem. Use the letters next to the problems to solve the riddle at the bottom of the page. Many letters will be used more than once while other letters will not be used at all.

H. 7 + (-5) = _____

Q. -8 + 4 = _____

D. 4 + (-6) = _____

B. -15 + (-3) = _____

F. -28 + 28 = _____

G. -9 – 2 = _____

O. 6 + (-9) = _____

W. -7 + (-8) = _____

K. -2 + (-4) = _____

X. -15 + (-6) = _____

S. -19 – (-18) = _____

A. 7 – 16 = _____

V. -2 – (-8) = _____

U. 8 – (-3) = _____

E. -9 + (-7) = _____

Y. -2 + 7 = _____

J. -18 + (-3) = _____

Z. (6 - 2) – (-4) = _____

C. 5 x 3 – (8 – 6) = _____

N. 6 – [2 – (-3)] = _____

M. 6 + [2 – (-4)] = _____

I . 10 + 22 + (-7) + (-30) = _____

P. -31 + 62 + (-9) = _____

T. 9 + 24 + (-5) + (-25) = _____

R. -5 + (-6) + (-9) = _____

L. -20 + (-19) – 2 = _____

Why did the dentist decide to join the army?

___ ___   ___ ___ ___ ___ ___ ___ ___
 2   -16   3   2   -3   11 -11 2   3

___ ___   ___ ___ ___ ___ ___
 2   -16   -15 -3   11 -41 -2

___ ___   ___   ___ ___ ___ ___
-18 -16   -9   -11 -3 -3 -2

___ ___ ___ ___ ___
-2 -20 -5 -41 -41

___ ___ ___ ___ ___ ___ ___ ___.
-1 -16 -20 -11 -16 -9   1   3

Sentence Variety

Directions: In order to achieve sentence variety, change the order of the words in the following sentences without changing the meanings. Insert commas where they are needed.

Example: I strolled to the neighborhood supermarket this morning to buy some milk.

This morning, I strolled to the neighborhood supermarket to buy some milk.

1. Do not go into the classroom unless you have permission first.

   _____

   _____

2. Henri could not go to the baseball game because he had the measles.

   _____

   _____

3. After the campers finished eating the hot dogs and marshmallows they roasted over the fire, they sat around telling ghost stories.

   _____

   _____

4. Louise picked up about twelve pounds of rocks when she went walking on Mora Beach.

   _____

   _____

5. Some of the banana slugs in the Hoh Rain Forest on the Olympic Peninsula are a foot long.

   _____

   _____

6. Before Tina could go to the movies, she had to wash the dishes, finish her homework, and clean her room.

   _____

   _____

7. Nearly every day, Fiona walks to school with her brother Ewan.

   _____

   _____

8. Every Tuesday from two until four in the afternoon, I practice playing the piano.

   _____

   _____

Signed Numbers

Directions: Compute the positive and negative values indicated in the problems below. Use the number line to help you with the easier amounts. Remember, always start at **0**. Go to the right for positive values. Go to the left for negative values.

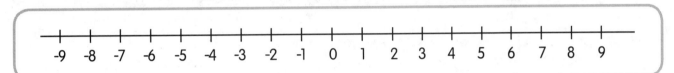

1. You have no money. You owe $4 to your best friend. You earn $5 doing chores. How much money will you have after you pay your friend? _____

2. John has no money, and he owes $9 to his brother. He receives $10 for his birthday. How much money does he have after paying back his brother? _____

3. Elizabeth has no money. She owes $7 to Michelle and $4 to Christine. How much money does she owe altogether? _____

4. What is the sum of -9 and 16? _____

5. James has no money, and he owes $9 to Ronny and $12 to Melissa. How much money does he owe altogether? _____

6. What is the sum of -10 and 12? _____

7. Irene has $15 but she owes $21 to her friend. How much money will she still owe if she gives the money that she has to her friend? _____

8. What is the sum of -7 and -17? _____

9. George scored 9 points in one game and 8 points in a second game. What was his point total? _____

10. What is the sum of -30 and -42? _____

11. What is the sum of -19 and -13? _____

12. Allison owes $87 to the bank and $139 to the credit card company. How much money does she owe altogether? _____

TV Guide

Directions: A TV guide is a list of programs arranged according to when they are aired. Use the *Pacific Post TV Guide* to answer the questions below.

Saturday, January 22		Pacific Post TV Guide	
ABN		**NTV**	**SBV**
Noon Sports World (includes reports from today's tennis, golf, bowling, and horse racing)	**Noon** Midday Movie: Class of '10 (G)	**Noon** Stage Divers (PG)
	2:00 State Athletics: Championships	**1:00** Report from Britain (RPT)
3:00 News Update		**2:30** Sky Devils (G)
3:15 Sports World		**3:00** Top Golf Courses
	4:00 Lost in Space (RPT)	**4:00** Theater News (G)
5:00 News and Weather		**5:00** Pet Hotline (G)
5:30 What's Cooking? (G)	**5:30** News and Weather	**5:30** Cartoon Break (Y)
	6:00 Sports Review	**6:00** News and Weather
6:30 Wildlife Park (G)	**6:30** Holiday Line (G)	**6:30** Just Stop It! (G)
7:30 Police Squad (RPT)	**7:30** Our Street (Y)	**7:30** Explorer Lost (G)
8:30 Art Report (MA)	**8:30** Night Train (PG)	**8:30** Movie: Ozone (PG)

Programs   Y — All Children   PG — Parental Guidance   RPT — Repeat
               G — General Audience   MA — Mature Audience   S — Subtitles

1. Which channel has news at 3 p.m.? _____   2. How long is *Our Street* on NTV? _____

3. Is *Art Report* suitable for children? _____   4. Which channel has the most sports? _____

5. What does "RPT" stand for? _____

6. How many parental guidance shows are scheduled to air? _____

7. Name a program that requires parental guidance. _____

8. If I watched *Police Squad*, I would miss *Night Train*.   ☐ True   ☐ False

9. The first full evening news report is on at 5:30 p.m.   ☐ True   ☐ False

10. The *Sports World* program is interrupted by a *News Update*.   ☐ True   ☐ False

11. What program might I watch to find out about caring for pets? _____

12. This guide was published in a paper. Which paper? _____

13. What day is this program for? _____

14. What show follows the NTV *Sports Review*? _____

Multiplying with Signed Numbers

Directions: Compute the positive and negative values indicated in the problems below.

> ### Formulas
>
> ☼ negative x negative = positive
>
> ☼ positive x negative = negative
>
> ☼ negative ÷ negative = positive
>
> ☼ positive ÷ negative = negative
>
> ☼ negative ÷ positive = negative

1. Jill owes $4 to Jennifer, $4 to Michelle, and $4 to Eileen. How much does she owe altogether?

   _____

2. Joey owes $5 to 4 different friends. How much money does he owe altogether?

   _____

3. What is the product of –7 and –6? _____

4. The total bill at a restaurant was $49 to be split evenly among 7 friends. How much money did each friend owe? _____

5. How much is –81 divided by 9? _____

6. How much is –100 divided by –10? _____

7. Each of 18 patrons owes $15 at a restaurant. What is the total amount owed by all 18 customers? _____

8. What is the product of –12 and –13? _____

9. How much is –16 times 4? _____

10. What is the quotient when –45 is divided by –9? _____

11. A group of 15 teenagers owes $75 at a pizza parlor. If they split the bill evenly, how much will each person owe? _____

12. How much is –200 divided by –10? _____

Cause and Effect

Directions: Complete the chart below. The left side of the chart is for causes, and the right side of the chart is for effects. Make sure that your answers make sense.

Causes	Effects
1. I tripped on the steps at school.	1. _____ _____ _____ _____
2. _____ _____ _____ _____	2. We were soaking wet!
3. I scored the winning goal in our soccer game.	3. _____ _____ _____ _____
4. _____ _____ _____ _____	4. My mom is very happy today.
5. I completed my homework.	5. _____ _____ _____ _____

If True, Then Do

Directions: To solve the puzzle and find the hidden word, read the sentences below. If the statement is true, color the numbered puzzle spaces as directed.

2	9	12	2	5	13	10 / 3		6	5	2	14	9 / 1
14 / 4	11	14	8	6	10	13	11	1	12 / 6 9	4	6
								9			
12	1	2	12	6	5	10	6	14		2	9
8	4	14	9	13	3	5	8	7	5	12	7
14	2	8	11	3	10	1	4	11	9	14	1

☼ If Mississippi is an ocean, color the #1 spaces blue.

☼ If Tennessee is a state, color the #2 spaces red.

☼ If Hawaii is a state, color the #3 spaces blue.

☼ If Mexico is a country, color the #4 spaces red.

☼ If Michigan is a country, color the #5 spaces red.

☼ If Florida is a river, color the #6 spaces blue.

☼ If Kentucky is in South America, color the #7 spaces red.

☼ If Canada is a country, color the #8 spaces red.

☼ If England is a continent, color the #9 spaces blue.

☼ If Washington is a state, color the #10 spaces blue.

☼ If Ohio is an island, color the #11 spaces blue.

☼ If New York is a city, color the #12 spaces red.

☼ If California borders an ocean, color the #13 spaces blue.

☼ If Australia is an island, color the #14 spaces red.

What word did you find?

_____

Sports Stumpers II

Directions: Find the name of the football, basketball, baseball, or hockey team that fits each clue. Choose your answer from the Team List.

Team List

A's	Dodgers	Saints
Avalanche	49ers	Sharks
Bears	Lightning	Timberwolves
Bulls	Patriots	Twins

1. This team is proud to be American. _____

2. This team looks like another team. _____

3. This team travels in packs. _____

4. This team can bury you alive. _____

5. This team has a lot of believers. _____

6. This team moves quickly. _____

7. This team loves the water. _____

8. This team might have cubs. _____

9. Each year, this team runs through the streets of Spain. _____

10. This team is friends with thunder. _____

11. This team gets good grades. _____

12. This team is always looking for gold. _____

Order of Operations

Directions: Evaluate the expressions. Be sure to follow the order of operations listed below. The first one has been done for you.

> ### Reminder
>
> Evaluate expressions in this order: **PEMDAS**
>
> ✿ **P**arentheses: Do these operations first.
>
> ✿ **E**xponents: Find these values next.
>
> ✿ **M**ultiply and **D**ivide: Go in order from left to right.
>
> ✿ **A**dd and **S**ubtract: Go in order from left to right.

1. $4^2 + 9 - (3 \times 5)$

   $4^2 + 9 - 15$

   $16 + 9 - 15$

   $25 - 15 = 10$

   _____10_____

2. $6^2 - (9 \times 2) + 12$

   _____

3. $10 + (8 \times 3) - 3^2$

   _____

4. $(8 \times 8) - 4^3 + 1$

   _____

5. $8^2 + (4 \times 5) - 21$

   _____

6. $(9 \times 5) - 2^3 + 16$

   _____

7. $15 \div 5 + 7 - 2^2$

   _____

8. $(9 + 11) - 3^2 + 7$

   _____

9. $(6 \times 5) - 14 - 4^2$

   _____

10. $12^2 - 9 \times 12 - 4^2$

    _____

11. $13^2 - (11 \times 9) + 16$

    _____

12. $13 + (6 \times 8) - 5^2$

    _____

13. $17 - (9 + 8) + 2^3$

    _____

14. $9^2 - (27 + 13) - 6^2$

    _____

15. $44 - 7 \times 6 + 4^2$

    _____

Word Choice

Writing

Directions: Replace the underlined words with more appropriate or more specific words. The first one has been done for you.

1. Sanford <u>said</u> that he would be <u>there</u> later.

   <u>Sanford growled that he would be at Commonwealth Park later.</u>

2. Josefina <u>liked</u> the <u>dress</u>.

   _____

3. Betty <u>walked</u> to the <u>store</u>.

   _____

4. The <u>music</u> was <u>terrific</u>.

   _____

5. Lim asked the <u>man</u> for <u>food</u>.

   _____

6. Beverly <u>ate</u> three <u>sandwiches</u>.

   _____

7. <u>Several children</u> skipped happily <u>away</u>.

   _____

8. Suzi thanked <u>her</u> <u>nicely</u>.

   _____

9. The <u>horse</u> <u>ran</u> around the corral.

   _____

10. Nolan <u>talked</u> with the <u>pretty</u> fashion model.

    _____

11. Because he did not want to be late for <u>the important occasion</u>, he <u>ran</u>.

    _____

Perimeter of Polygons

Directions: Compute the perimeter of the shapes below.

> **Reminder**
>
> The perimeter of a parallelogram is computed by adding the length plus the width and multiplying the sum by two.
>
> Perimeter of a parallelogram = 2 x (length + width)

1.

25 yds.

40 yds.

_____

2.

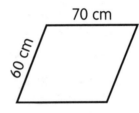

70 cm

60 cm

_____

3.

95 ft.

70 ft.

_____

4.

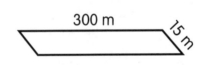

300 m

15 m

_____

5.

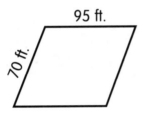

45 cm

80 cm

_____

6.

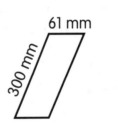

61 mm

300 mm

_____

7.

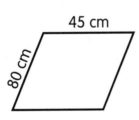

90.2 m

20.3 m

_____

8.

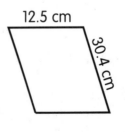

12.5 cm

30.4 cm

_____

The Birds

Directions: Read the passage, and then circle the correct answers below.

There once was a farmer who planted fresh fields of wheat. He cared for the wheat and ensured that it received adequate amounts of water, sun, and nourishment. His livelihood depended on this crop of wheat.

One morning, the farmer awoke to the sound of birds in his field. He ran outside and saw his wheat field covered with birds. In a panic, he ran outside and began flapping his arms and making loud sounds. He hoped that this would scare the birds away. His plan worked. The birds flew away in a flurry, and the farmer went back about his work.

Early the next morning, the farmer was again awakened to the sound of birds. He followed the same procedure and scared the birds by making loud noises and flapping his arms. It worked again. The birds flew away and left his wheat alone.

The birds began to realize that they were never in any real danger. They realized the farmer walked around waving at them and making sounds. The birds got braver and braver.

On the third morning, the farmer heard the birds again and realized that he needed to be more severe. He grabbed his dog's collar and headed outside. The birds did not even move. They knew he would try to scare them, so they weren't too worried. The farmer let his dog loose, and the dog chased the birds. This frightened the birds, and they flew away, never to be seen again.

1. What is the moral of the story?

    a. What goes around comes around.

    b. Work before play.

    c. If at first you don't succeed, try, try again.

    d. The early bird gets the worm.

2. What would be a good title for this reading passage?

    a. "The Last Resort"

    b. "The Two Sides"

    c. "Planting Seeds"

    d. "Anger Always Works First"

3. Locate the statement below that did *not* happen in the story.

    a. The farmer was trying to attract the birds.

    b. The farmer wanted to delay hurting the birds.

    c. The farmer knew that he had to show the birds he meant business.

    d. The birds were not afraid of the farmer.

Area

Directions: Lawn Magic is a business run by three sixth-grade friends who earn money mowing their neighbors' lawns. They charge by the square foot, so they need to know the area of each lawn they mow. Help Lawn Magic compute the area in square feet of each lawn described below.

Formulas

☼ Area of a rectangle = base x height (or length x width)

☼ Area of a parallelogram = base x height

☼ Area of a triangle = base x height ÷ 2

---

1. Lawn Magic did your neighbor's lawn, which is a rectangular shape 12 feet high and 20 feet long at the base. What is the area? _____ square feet

2. Lawn Magic mowed Mr. Crick's parallelogram-shaped lawn, which has a height of 15 feet and a base of 30 feet. What is the area? _____ square feet

3. Mr. Ford's lawn is a parallelogram with a height of 23 feet and a base of 45 feet. What is the area Lawn Magic will mow? _____ square feet

4. Mrs. Jopp's lawn is triangular with a height of 12 feet and a base of 40 feet. What is the area that Lawn Magic will mow? _____ square feet

5. Lawn Magic mowed Mr. Lee's front lawn, which is a rectangle 43 feet high and 97 feet at the base. What is the area they mowed? _____ square feet

6. Mr. Dapper's back lawn is a triangle with a height of 33 feet and a base of 70 feet. What is the area? _____ square feet

7. Mrs. Smith's side lawn is a parallelogram 22.4 feet high and 30 feet at the base. What is the area Lawn Magic will mow? _____ square feet

8. Lawn Magic mowed Ms. Brown's front lawn, a triangle 12.5 feet high and 14 feet at the base. What is the area they mowed? _____ square feet

9. What is the area of a triangular lawn 16.6 feet high and 12 feet at the base? _____ square feet

10. What is the area of a square lawn 22 feet on each side? _____ square feet

---

Irregular Verbs

Many verbs end in *-ed* when you put them into the past tense. However, for some verbs, you do not simply add an *-ed* to put them into past tense. These are called irregular verbs. Here are some examples:

Present tense	Past tense
spy	spied
hide	hid
bring	brought

Part I

Directions: Write the following irregular verbs in the past tense.

1. fly _____
2. swim _____
3. cry _____
4. drink _____
5. go _____
6. speed _____

7. run _____
8. sing _____
9. draw _____
10. eat _____
11. buy _____
12. speak _____

13. ride _____
14. wear _____
15. grow _____
16. freeze _____
17. make _____
18. sleep _____

Part II

Sometimes, other words in the sentence can give clues as to which tense the verb should be in. Words such as *yesterday, last month,* and *previously* show that the action occurred in the past. Words such as *tomorrow, in the future,* and *next week* show that the action will occur in the future.

Directions: Add a verb to each of the sentences below. Make sure your choice is in the appropriate tense.

1. Last week, we _____ to the opera.

2. Today, I _____ exhausted, and I can't stop yawning.

3. In 2010, my family _____ a huge party.

4. Riley _____ when I say, "You know?"

5. Jesse James _____ in his farmhouse in the late 1800s.

6. Tomorrow, we _____ to the movies.

7. In the year 3000, people _____ on Mars.

8. Yesterday, I _____ twenty dollars.

Finding the Volume

Part I

Directions: Find the volume for each rectangular solid.

> **Formula**
>
> Volume of a rectangular solid = length x width x height
>
> V = l x w x h

1.

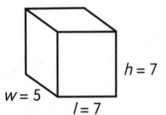

w = 5
l = 7
h = 7

_____ x _____ x _____ =

_____ cubic units

2.

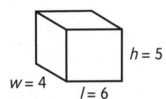

w = 4
l = 6
h = 5

_____ x _____ x _____ =

_____ cubic units

3.

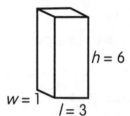

w = 1
l = 3
h = 6

_____ x _____ x _____ =

_____ cubic units

Part II

Directions: Find the volume for each cube.

> **Formula**
>
> Volume of a cube = side x side x side
>
> V = s³

1.

s = 1

_____³ = _____ cubic unit(s)

2.

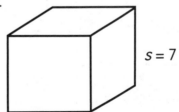

s = 7

_____³ = _____ cubic units

3.

s = 5

_____³ = _____ cubic units

Use Your Brain Power

Mini Dictionary

bunker — an underground shelter

cavalcade — a group of horse riders

correspondent — a reporter sent to a faraway place

despot — a ruler with absolute power

premiere — the first performance

testimony — a statement of facts

toupee — a man's wig

tribulation — a lot of great troubles

Part I

Directions: Use the Mini Dictionary to help you answer the riddles below.

1. I am what the audience is waiting for. _____

2. I am someone the people might fear. _____

3. I am sometimes a part of a parade. _____

4. I am a challenge to your patience and courage. _____

5. I could be a part of a costume. _____

6. I can be a soldier's defense. _____

7. I am the words from a witness to a crime. _____

8. I relay current information. _____

Part II

Directions: Fill in each sentence with the best word from the Mini Dictionary.

1. The group planned a revolution to overthrow the _____ .

2. He escaped injury by crawling into a _____ .

3. The tickets for the play's _____ were quite expensive.

4. Grampa doesn't allow anyone to play with the _____ on his head.

5. Much of the _____ in the world is caused by wars.

6. The sight of the _____ entertained the crowd.

7. She is based in London as a television _____ .

8. It is illegal to lie during _____ in a court of law.

Homophone Word Search

Directions: In the puzzle below, find the homophones for the given words. The first one has been done for you.

~~all~~	eight	new	pole
allowed	fawn	no	ring
capitol	hymn	not	sight/site
cell	knight	our	sun
do/due	male	pale	tide

```
A  W  L  F  U  L  H  O  U  R  A  N
F  A  U  N  M  A  N  G  K  N  O  T
A  N  N  U  A  R  Y  I  S  S  T  L
D  I  P  S  I  C  A  P  I  T  A  L
A  G  I  T  L  K  N  E  W  A  G  H
A  H  P  H  E  N  D  R  I  A  S  T
R  T  K  A  T  E  I  B  B  B  E  E
A  P  N  N  I  N  N  P  P  O  L  L
L  L  O  L  G  L  O  O  G  L  L  C
O  W  W  R  N  G  G  H  H  Y  Y  I
U  E  V  R  E  S  T  I  E  D  A  T
D  X  M  C  S  T  U  M  I  N  G  E
```

Homophone Crossword

Directions: Write the homophones for the given words in the puzzle below.

Across

2. ate
5. chili
6. piece
7. plumb
11. forth
13. vein/vane
15. write/rite
16. maid
17. paws

Down

1. bin
3. tow
4. wood
5. sense/scents
6. pour/pore
7. principle
8. knight
9. borne
10. their/they're
12. patients
14. sail

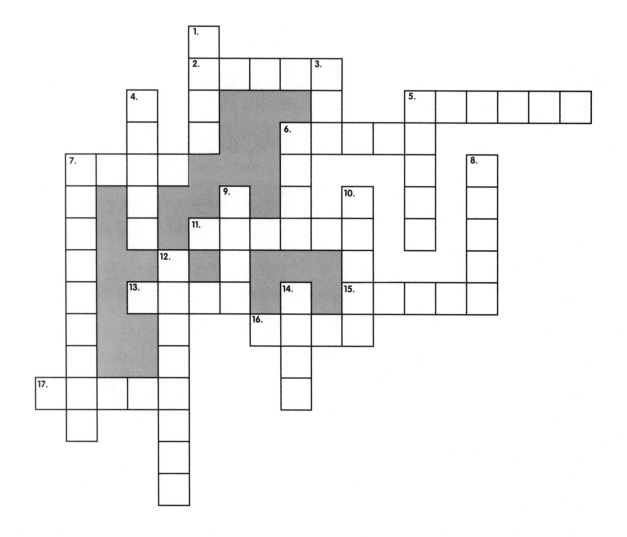

Geometry

Directions: Read each problem carefully. Circle the correct answer.

1. What are these lines called?

    a. intersecting

    b. parallel

    c. perpendicular

    d. crossing

2. What are these lines called?

    a. parallel

    b. perpendicular

    c. crossing

    d. segments

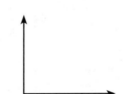

3. What kind of angle is this?

    a. obtuse

    b. acute

    c. 30 degree

    d. right

4. Which angle is less than 90 degrees?

    a. obtuse

    b. right

    c. acute

    d. sharp

5. What is the name of this angle?

    a. <DEF

    b. <EFD

    c. <FED

    d. both a and c

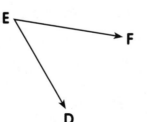

6. Two angles that add up to 180 degrees are called what?

    a. supplementary

    b. complementary

    c. both of these

    d. none of these

7. What kind of a triangle is this?

    a. isosceles

    b. scalene

    c. equilateral

    d. none of these

8. What defines a scalene triangle?

    a. It has two sides of equal length.

    b. It has three sides of equal length.

    c. It is pointy.

    d. It has no sides of equal length.

9. What is this called?

    a. ray line

    b. line

    c. line segment

    d. end point

10. What kinds of lines are these?

    a. adjacent

    b. intersecting

    c. infinity

    d. perpendicular

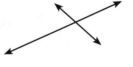

The Nile in Ancient Egypt

Directions: Read the passage below, and then circle the correct answers.

Ancient Egyptian life centered around the life-giving waters of the Nile, the longest river in the world. Every Egyptian, from the poorest peasant to the pharaoh, depended on the Nile, as its banks contained the only land with soil able to grow crops.

The Egyptians took full advantage of the Nile River. People were able to live secure in the knowledge that they were safe from intruders who didn't dare cross the deserts that surrounded their fertile valleys. Because of the annual flooding, the Egyptians were able to establish a fairly regular cycle of planting and harvesting. Excess crops were then exported, making Egypt a wealthy nation. Animals thrived in the waters and surrounding land of the Nile. Goods were easily transported on barges and ferries. Probably the most valuable gift of the Nile was papyrus, a tall reed which grew along its banks. Papyrus was used to make paper, and Egypt was the sole supplier of this product until rag paper was invented in the twelfth century.

1. Who depended on the Nile?

    a. the pharaoh   c. the peasants

    b. the farmers   d. all of the above

2. According to the passage, what did the Nile do that helped the Egyptians establish a farming cycle?

    a. It ran into channels they had created to water their crops.

    b. It flooded each year.

    c. It dried out each year, so the farmers could use the riverbed for farming.

    d. It kept the farm animals alive.

3. According to the passage, how did the Nile help make the Egyptians wealthy?

    a. The Egyptians could produce enough crops to sell to other countries.

    b. The Egyptians could produce enough crops to feed their families.

    c. The Egyptians could pan for gold in the Nile.

    d. The Egyptians bottled the water from the Nile and sold it.

4. According to the passage, the most valuable gift of the Nile was probably

    a. water.

    b. the animals who lived on the Nile.

    c. papyrus.

    d. the crops that the Nile produced.

Cartesian Coordinates

Directions: *How do you make a hot dog stand?* The answer to this riddle is written in a special code at the bottom of this page. Each pair of numbers stands for a point on the graph. Write the letter shown near the point at the intersection of each pair of numbers. Read numbers across and then up. The letters will spell out the answer to the riddle.

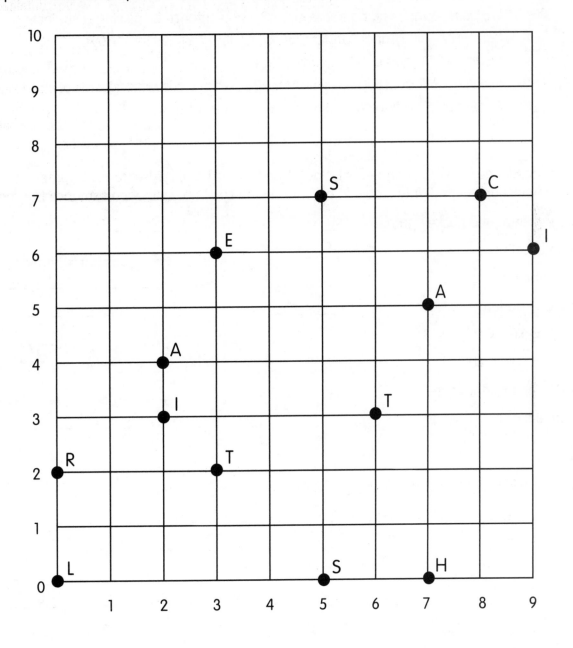

____ ____ ____ ____ ____   ____ ____ ____   ____ ____ ____ ____ ____.

(5, 7) (6, 3) (3, 6) (7, 5) (0, 0)   (2, 3) (3, 2) (5, 0)   (8, 7) (7, 0) (2, 4) (9, 6) (0, 2)

Sentence Fragments

Sentence fragments occur when a sentence is missing either a subject or a verb. Sentence fragments are also called incomplete sentences.

Examples: *Incorrect*—Going to the circus tomorrow.

Problem—Who is going to the circus? The sentence is missing a subject.

Correction—Judy and Flanders are going to the circus tomorrow.

Incorrect—My two cats, Iago and Alger.

Problem—What action is occurring? The sentence is missing a verb.

Correction—My two cats, Iago and Alger, love to sleep.

Part I

Directions: Study the sentence fragments below. Decide whether each sentence fragment is missing a subject or a verb. Write "subject" or "verb" in the space beside each sentence fragment.

1. Are watching the hockey game. _____

2. Is an excellent actress. _____

3. Can juggle six apples. _____

4. The old, battered suitcase. _____

5. Los Angeles, California. _____

6. The red convertible. _____

7. Is studying earthquakes. _____

8. Mother's antique dishes. _____

Part II

Directions: Now, rewrite each fragment, adding either a subject or a verb to make a complete sentence.

1. _____

2. _____

3. _____

4. _____

5. _____

6. _____

7. _____

8. _____

Identifying Coordinate Points

Directions: Write the coordinate for each point.

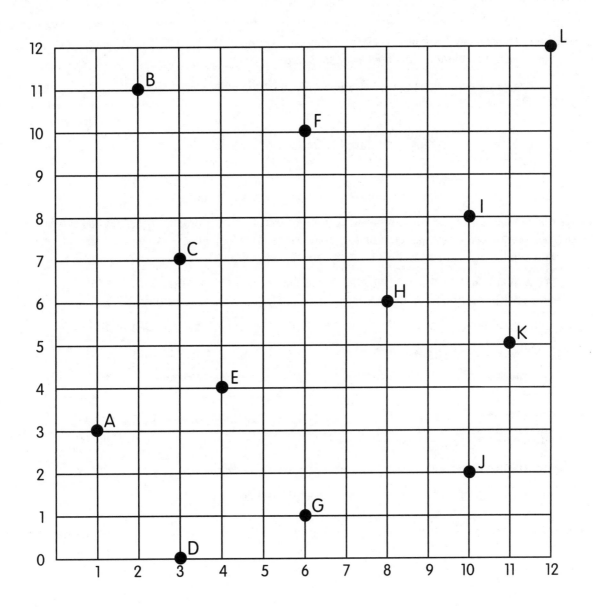

1. K = _____   4. L = _____   7. H = _____   10. C = _____

2. D = _____   5. E = _____   8. B = _____   11. A = _____

3. G = _____   6. I = _____   9. F = _____   12. J = _____

The Green Revolution

Directions: This passage is an excerpt from the book *Earth First* by David Bowden and Jenny Dibley. Read the passage, and then answer the questions below.

There is a revolution taking place in the minds of consumers around the world. It is known as the "green revolution" or the era of environmentally-friendly shopping.

In the past, many consumers have not given their shopping habits and choices much thought. The need to think about what happens to products when they have been used has not, until recently, been an issue of concern.

In the past few years, however, consumers have become much more conscious of the impact of their shopping habits. People are now discussing the environment in terms of how everyone has a role to play in reversing this damage. Every time we buy a product, we consume resources that in some way deplete the environment. This is why it is time to rethink our shopping habits and choices.

There are many points to consider when buying a product. The cost of a product is usually the most important consideration for consumers. Comfort, size, shape, how fashionable the product is, and how it compares with similar products in terms of quality, are also important.

The "green consumer" will also consider how the use of the product being purchased will affect the environment. Today's consumers should ask themselves the following questions before selecting a product:

- ☼ Has an animal suffered or died to make it?
- ☼ Were harmful chemicals used to make it?
- ☼ Is it overpackaged?
- ☼ Is it made from recycled materials?
- ☼ Can it be reused or recycled after it is used?
- ☼ Is it really necessary?

1. According to the excerpt, the "green revolution" is mainly concerned with

☐ the cost of goods in supermarkets.

☐ whether or not goods are made from recycled material.

☐ how the production of a product will affect the environment.

☐ the amount of unnecessary packaging on many items.

2. A "green consumer" is one who

☐ will not buy goods from a supermarket.

☐ considers many points before making a purchase.

☐ reuses all the packaging that comes with a purchase.

☐ will only damage the environment if the goods are not expensive.

3. For some shoppers, fashion is more important than the environment. ☐ True ☐ False

4. Which bullet point would you consider most important when you go shopping? Why?

_____

_____

Dividing Fractions

Directions: Divide the fractions below. Write your answers in lowest terms.

1. $3\frac{2}{3} \div 4\frac{2}{3} =$

2. $4\frac{3}{7} \div 2\frac{4}{7} =$

3. $2\frac{1}{3} \div 3\frac{1}{6} =$

4. $5\frac{6}{7} \div 6\frac{3}{14} =$

5. $3\frac{3}{5} \div 5\frac{4}{5} =$

6. $\frac{5}{6} \div \frac{2}{3} =$

7. $\frac{1}{4} \div \frac{3}{8} =$

8. $\frac{5}{12} \div \frac{2}{24} =$

9. $\frac{3}{10} \div \frac{12}{30} =$

10. $\frac{1}{5} \div \frac{4}{15} =$

11. $\frac{13}{20} \div \frac{3}{10} =$

12. $\frac{2}{7} \div \frac{2}{3} =$

13. $\frac{1}{6} \div \frac{2}{5} =$

14. $\frac{4}{9} \div \frac{1}{2} =$

15. $\frac{8}{9} \div \frac{3}{4} =$

16. $\frac{3}{6} \div 1\frac{2}{3} =$

17. $2\frac{1}{3} \div \frac{3}{4} =$

18. $3\frac{3}{4} \div \frac{3}{5} =$

19. $6\frac{1}{2} \div \frac{2}{3} =$

20. $1\frac{1}{2} \div 6 =$

21. $\frac{5}{7} \div 3\frac{4}{5} =$

22. $\frac{1}{4} \div 3\frac{1}{5} =$

23. $2\frac{3}{8} \div \frac{4}{5} =$

24. $3\frac{3}{4} \div \frac{1}{9} =$

Adjectives

Adjectives are words that describe either nouns or pronouns. They answer these questions: *What kind? How many? Which one? How much?*

Examples: She wore a *silver* ring on her finger. (*What kind?*)

We served dinner to *forty* people. (*How many?*)

Thomas gave a dollar to the *homeless* man on the corner. (*Which one?*)

I need to buy *three boxes* of sugar. (*How much?*)

Part I

Directions: Rewrite the following sentences, adding adjectives to answer the questions.

1. Georgina likes her dance class. (*What kind?*)

   _____

2. People crowded into the stadium for the concert. (*How many?*)

   _____

3. I won the stuffed bear. (*Which one?*)

   _____

4. Mickey did math homework. (*How much?*)

   _____

There are three types of adjectives:

☼ Common adjectives describe nouns or pronouns.

   Example: The *strong* woman lifted boxes into the truck.

☼ Proper adjectives are formed from proper nouns.

   Example: She studied *Egyptian* art in college.

☼ Compound adjectives are made up of more than one word. They are sometimes hyphenated.

   Examples: My brother lives in a *far-off* place.

Part II

Directions: Add adjectives to the sentences below, according to the type listed after each sentence.

1. My _____ brother hates avocados and tomatoes. (*common adjective*)

2. Pizza and lasagna are Jake's favorite types of _____ food. (*proper adjective*)

3. Tom found a _____ clover. (*compound adjective*)

4. Every summer, we go to the _____ Ocean. (*proper adjective*)

5. Her _____ dress cost twenty dollars. (*common adjective*)

6. Janice's _____ daughter will be driving soon. (*compound adjective*)

Apartment Living

Directions: Find each person's apartment and write it on the lines.

Clues

- ✿ Brandon lives directly across from Matt and in between Violet and Maria.
- ✿ Louisa lives in an even-numbered apartment.
- ✿ Gary lives directly across from Violet and next door to a boy.
- ✿ Maria lives directly across from a girl.
- ✿ Brandon lives in an odd-numbered apartment.
- ✿ Maria lives in apartment number 215.

210	212	214

211	213	215

Matt lives in apartment number _____ .

Brandon lives in apartment number_____ .

Gary lives in apartment number_____ .

Louisa lives in apartment number _____ .

Maria lives in apartment number_____ .

Violet lives in apartment number _____ .

More Map Madness!

Do you see Juanita? She is lost again! Follow the directions to get her back on track. Mark her ending spot with an **X**.

Directions:

1. Take Hennepin Ave. southwest.

2. Turn left just after the City Shopping Center.

3. Turn left on 2nd Ave. S.

4. Go east on E. 3rd St.

5. Turn right on S. 5th Ave.

6. **END** End at the corner of E. 8th St.

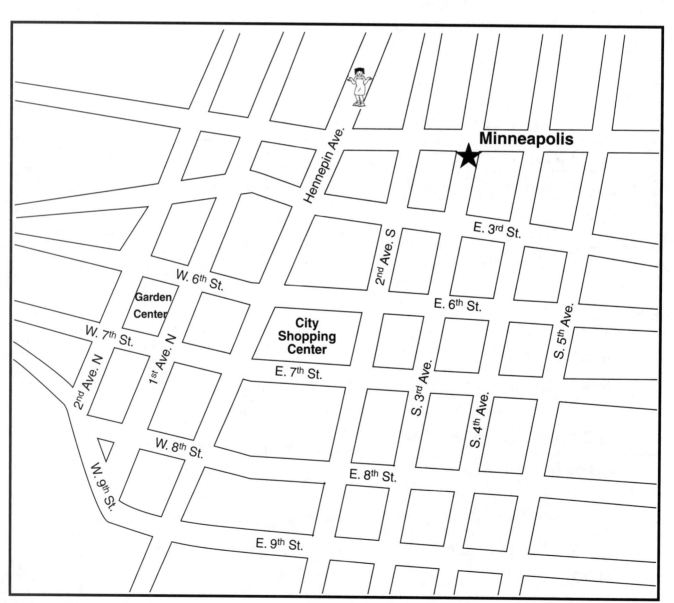

Common Multiples and Factors

Directions: Read each problem carefully. Circle the correct answer. *Hint:* LCM means Lowest Common Multiple, and GCF means Greatest Common Factor.

Examples

1. Find the LCM of 5 and 12.
   - a. 16
   - (b.) 60
   - c. 24
   - d. 120

2. Find the GCF of 20 and 30.
   - (a.) 10
   - b. 20
   - c. 1
   - d. 2

---

1. Find the GCF of 8 and 40.
   - a. 10
   - b. 9
   - c. 8
   - d. none of the above

2. Find the LCM of 8 and 10.
   - a. 10
   - b. 40
   - c. 36
   - d. 80

3. Find the GCF of 12 and 27.
   - a. 4
   - b. 9
   - c. 6
   - d. 3

4. Find the LCM of 7 and 9.
   - a. 7
   - b. 9
   - c. 54
   - d. 63

5. Find the GCF of 48 and 36.
   - a. 9
   - b. 16
   - c. 12
   - d. none of the above

6. Find the GCF of 8 and 27.
   - a. 1
   - b. 4
   - c. 8
   - d. 7

7. Find the LCM of 3 and 15.
   - a. 15
   - b. 30
   - c. 12
   - d. 21

8. Find the LCM of 9 and 20.
   - a. 150
   - b. 167
   - c. 180
   - d. 20

Adverbs

Adverbs are words that describe verbs, adjectives, or other adverbs. They answer these questions: *When? To what extent? How?*

Examples: My father ran *yesterday.* (*When?*)

Maribelle sang *badly.* (*How?*)

She *partially* finished her homework. (*To what extent?*)

Most adverbs are formed by adding *-ly* to an adjective. Here are some examples:

Adjective	Adverb
soft	softly
sad	sadly
beautiful	beautifully
quick	quickly
mad	madly

Other adverbs do not end in *-ly.* Some examples are *already, often, far, now, more,* and *soon.*

Part I

Directions: Rewrite the following sentences, adding adverbs to answer the questions below.

1. The monkey did tricks for the crowd. (*When?*)

_____

2. The teacher gave the instructions. (*How?*)

_____

3. I ate my dinner. (*To what extent?*)

_____

Part II

Directions: Add adverbs to the sentences below to correspond with the question after each sentence.

1. I _____ understand your argument. (*To what extent?*)

2. We're moving to a new city _____ . (*When?*)

3. My older brother sings _____ in the shower. (*How?*)

4. The tree fell _____ . (*How?*)

Fractions and Mixed Operations

Directions: Candy Is Dandy is a special candy store with trays of Lick 'em Lollipops, Nutty Buddies, Chocolate P and Ps, Jelly Smellies, Luscious Licorice, Geodesic Gumballs, Choco-Nuts, and Slurpy Suckers. Use your knowledge of fractions to help Candy Is Dandy serve its customers.

1. Your mother bought $\frac{1}{3}$ of a pound of Jelly Smellies and $\frac{1}{4}$ of a pound of Geodesic Gumballs. How many pounds of candy did she buy? _____

2. The school principal bought $\frac{3}{4}$ of a pound of Nutty Buddies, and the second-grade teacher bought $\frac{2}{3}$ of a pound of Nutty Buddies. How many pounds of Nutty Buddies did they buy in all? _____

3. Your best friend bought $\frac{7}{8}$ of a pound of Slurpy Suckers. The school quarterback bought $\frac{3}{4}$ of a pound of Slurpy Suckers. How much more did your best friend buy? _____

4. The soccer coach bought $\frac{11}{12}$ of a pound of Choco-Nuts. The basketball coach bought $\frac{5}{6}$ of a pound of the same candy. How much more did the soccer coach buy? _____

5. Candy Is Dandy is selling Chocolate P and Ps in baggies that hold $\frac{1}{3}$ of a pound. Robert bought 15 bags of Chocolate P and Ps. How many pounds of candy did he buy? _____

6. Chris bought $\frac{3}{4}$ of a foot of Luscious Licorice. James only bought $\frac{1}{3}$ as much licorice as Chris. How much licorice did James buy? _____

7. Christine bought $\frac{9}{10}$ of a pound of Chocolate P and Ps and $\frac{4}{5}$ of a pound of Choco-Nuts. How much candy did she buy altogether? _____

8. Sarah bought $\frac{1}{8}$ of a foot of Luscious Licorice and Angela bought $\frac{7}{12}$ of a foot of Luscious Licorice. How much less did Sarah buy? _____

9. Anthony bought $\frac{3}{4}$ of a pound of Chocolate P and Ps, which he split evenly into cups holding $\frac{1}{8}$ of a pound. How many cups did he have? _____

10. Michael bought $\frac{1}{2}$ of a pound of Nutty Buddies, $\frac{4}{5}$ of a pound of Geodesic Gumballs, and $\frac{1}{3}$ of a pound of Slurpy Suckers. How many pounds of candy did he buy altogether?

_____

Mission to Mars

Directions: Read the passage, and then circle the correct answers.

On July 4, 1997, space exploration took a huge step. On that day, a spacecraft called *Pathfinder* landed on Mars. The National Aeronautics and Space Administration (NASA) sent *Pathfinder* to discover new information about the Red Planet.

The mission was a complete success. After landing, *Pathfinder* sent a small rover, *Sojourner*, onto the planet's surface. *Sojourner* explored more than 250 square meters of Mars. Together, *Pathfinder* and *Sojourner* took more than 16,000 photos of the rocky landscape. Engineers designed *Sojourner* to last for only seven days, but the little vehicle ran twelve times longer! *Pathfinder* surprised scientists, too. It sent back information for almost three months. That was three times longer than it was built to last.

Because *Pathfinder* and *Sojourner* ran for so long, scientists got more information than they ever dreamed of getting. For one thing, they discovered that Mars is very sandy. Pictures of sand dunes around the landing site hint that Mars once had water. Scientists know that water means life. Was there ever life on Mars? We don't know yet.

In addition, the *Pathfinder* mission told scientists that Mars is dusty. Huge "dust devils" on Mars spit enormous amounts of dust into the Martian air. *Pathfinder* also recorded frosty Martian temperatures at 200°F below zero. At that temperature, a glass of water would freeze solid in just a few seconds.

In October, scientists lost *Pathfinder's* signal because the spacecraft's battery had run down. They tried to revive the signal but had no luck. The mission officially ended on November 4.

Scientists hope to use the knowledge from this mission to get a better understanding of how life on Earth began. They'll also use it to plan future Mars missions.

1. What did NASA do to get information about Mars?
    a. NASA sent the spacecraft *Sojourner* to Mars.
    b. NASA sent engineers on a three-month space mission.
    c. NASA sent the spacecraft *Pathfinder* to Mars.
    d. NASA sent astronauts to run tests for seven days.

2. What was the main reason NASA considered the *Pathfinder* mission a success?
    a. Scientists found out that Mars is very cold and dusty.
    b. Scientists got more information than they ever dreamed of getting.
    c. Scientists learned that Mars definitely had water at one time.
    d. Scientists found out that there was once life on Mars.

3. You can tell from this passage that
    a. dust devils on Mars made the photographs hard to see.
    b. Martian temperatures caused *Pathfinder's* battery to fail.
    c. scientists suspect that life on Earth began on Mars.
    d. scientists will look for signs that life existed on Mars.

Fractions, Decimals, Percents

Math

Part I

Directions: Some states require that out-of-state businesses pay a shipping tax to send goods to state residents. Refer to this table to do the problems below. (*Note:* The shipping rates do not reflect the actual current rates.)

Shipping Taxes

Alabama	AL	8.00%	Indiana	IN	5.00%
Maryland	MD	5.75%	Kentucky	KY	6.00%
Georgia	GA	4.00%	Missouri	MO	5.725%
Illinois	IL	2.00%			

1. Miguel lives in Maryland and purchased a sweater for $39.99 from a catalog. Add the shipping tax. What's the total cost of the sweater? _____

2. Mr. and Mrs. Wong paid a total of $200.00 for an entertainment center for their home in Chicago, Illinois. The salesperson said that a 2% shipping tax was already added to the final price. What was the price of the entertainment center before the tax was added? _____

3. The Williams family live in Lexington, Kentucky. They recently purchased a computer for $1,295.00. What is the total price for the computer after the shipping tax is added?

   _____

Part II

Directions: Complete the table below. Find the fraction, decimal, or percent equivalent to the one given.

	Fraction	Decimal	Percent
1.	$\frac{1}{10}$		
2.		.25	
3.			45%
4.			15%
5.	$\frac{4}{5}$		
6.	$\frac{7}{8}$		
7.		.77	
8.	$\frac{1}{20}$		
9.		.22	
10.			40%

Commas in a Series

Use a comma to separate three or more words in a series. The comma goes between words in a series. The "and" goes between the second to last word and the last word in the series.

Example: Manatees are slow, gentle, and curious creatures.

Directions: Use each set of words in a sentence. When appropriate, add commas and the word "and."

1. large   heavy   peaceful

_____

_____

2. grass   weeds   kelp

_____

_____

3. warm   calm   shallow

_____

_____

4. Gulf of Mexico   Florida   Caribbean Sea

_____

_____

5. newsletter   photo   certificate

_____

_____

6. scratched   cut   bruised

_____

_____

newspaper Graph

Directions: Look at the graph. Which statements below are true and which are false?

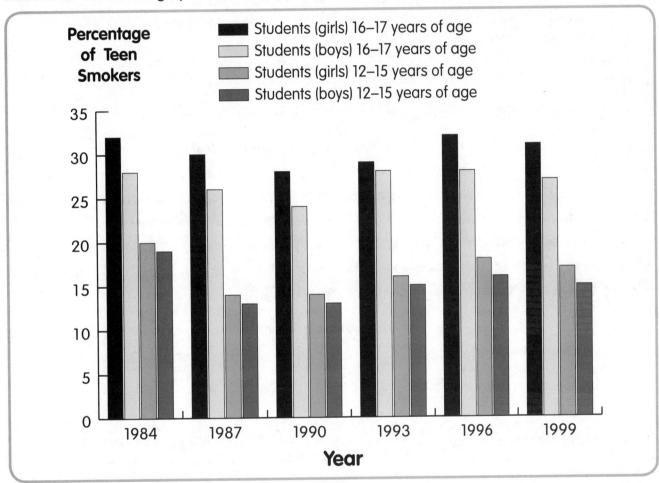

1. Youths 16–17 years old smoke more than youths 12–15 years old.   True / False

2. Boys of all ages smoke more than girls.   True / False

3. Boys aged 12–15 smoke more than girls aged 12–15 years old.   True / False

4. The lowest rate of smoking for 12–15 year olds was from 1987 to 1990.   True / False

5. Smoking by all groups has been declining since 1996.   True / False

6. In 1999, about 17% of boys aged 12–15 smoked.   True / False

7. In 1996, about 23% of boys aged 16–17 smoked.   True / False

8. The difference between boys' and girls' rates is greater for the older age group.   True / False

Short and Long

Punctuation Rule

Use quotation marks in writing titles of short works, such as magazine articles, short stories, poems, songs, and chapters of books.

Part I

Directions: Read the following paragraph. Insert quotation marks wherever needed.

My favorite poem, Love Is Alive, was written by American poet Sophie Harrington. I read anything written by or about her that I can find. I was especially happy to find that, in my subscription to *Grandeur*, there was an article entitled Up and Coming Poets that featured Sophie and her work. As I read the article, I was surprised to discover that she has also written several short stories. Her latest short story, The How and Why of It All, is scheduled to be in the next issue of *Grandeur*. Since I too am a writer, she has inspired me to begin writing a song that I've tentatively titled, My Inspiration. I may even send her a copy of it, once I have it completed. Hopefully she will reply, but if she doesn't, she is still my favorite writer.

Punctuation Rule

Use <u>underlining</u> or *italics* for titles of longer works, such as books, TV shows, movies, works of art, and the names of ships.

Part II

Directions: Match the following titles to each subject, and then use each title in a sentence.

1. *The Sound of Music*	TV show
2. *Titanic*	musical
3. *Hatchet*	ship
4. *The Simpsons*	book

1. _____

_____

2. _____

_____

3. _____

_____

4. _____

_____

Array Grid

Directions: Read each word in the boxes below. Cross out any word that is a number word. Take the first letter of each word that is left and write them in order on the lines below. The letters will spell the name of a famous scientist.

twenty	five	million	greater	hundredth
hundred	area	sixteen	dozen	trillion
length	century	decade	seventy	tenth
invert	fifty	zero	four	thirty
less	fifteen	equal	billion	thousand
seven	sixty	one-half	order	twelve

___ ___ ___ ___ ___ ___

Silly Sayings

Directions: Each box below contains a common saying. Study each box, and write the saying on the line.

lang4uage

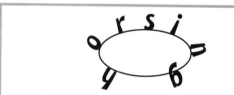

👁 CURYY4me

dice dice

---

k
c
e
h
c

---

sitting THE WORLD

mi1llion

Go *it it it it*

70

Understanding Graphs and Tables

Directions: Look at the graph below and answer the questions.

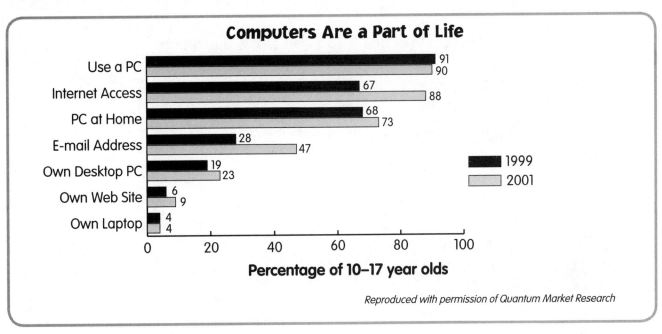

Computers Are a Part of Life

Use a PC — 91 (1999), 90 (2001)
Internet Access — 67 (1999), 88 (2001)
PC at Home — 68 (1999), 73 (2001)
E-mail Address — 28 (1999), 47 (2001)
Own Desktop PC — 19 (1999), 23 (2001)
Own Web Site — 6 (1999), 9 (2001)
Own Laptop — 4 (1999), 4 (2001)

■ 1999
▢ 2001

Percentage of 10–17 year olds

Reproduced with permission of Quantum Market Research

1. In which years was the research done? _____

2. Does the graph show what 10–17 year olds use computers for?_____

3. How many 10–17 year olds had Internet access in 2001?_____

4. Was this more or less than in 1999? _____ What was the difference between the two years?

   _____

5. What does the figure of 47 mean?_____

6. What increase is there over the two years in the percentage of 10–17 year olds who own their own desktop PC?_____

7. Does the graph indicate an increase or decrease overall in computer use over the two years studied? Explain your answer.

   _____

8. Think about what you know about computer use among your age group at the moment. Would you say that the figures for this year would be different from these or the same?

   _____

   In what ways? _____

The Best Definition

Directions: For each sentence below, choose the definition that matches the way the italicized word is used in the sentence.

1. Senator Whistler took the *floor* to defend his position on the immigration bill.
   a. to knock down
   b. upper or uppermost surface
   c. right to address an assembly

2. Professor Watkins went to Australia to participate in the *dig*.
   a. an archaeological site
   b. to learn or discover
   c. to break up, turn over, or remove

3. My vigorous friend Audrey was a *rock* and stayed with me the entire time.
   a. move back and forth; zigzag
   b. stable, firm, dependable one
   c. naturally formed mineral

4. Attorney William Joseph's *opposite* in the case was Attorney Justine Modigliani.
   a. one that is contrary to another
   b. located directly behind or ahead of
   c. sharply contrasting

5. Catherine Laws, my sixth-grade teacher, *holds* a degree in music also.
   a. to restrain; curb
   b. to have in one's possession
   c. to regard or consider

6. When we went sailing Saturday, the seas were very *heavy*.
   a. weighted down; burdened
   b. filling; hard to digest
   c. violent, rough

7. The argument between the two wealthy adversaries quickly became *heated*.
   a. warm a building
   b. degree of warmth or hotness
   c. intense, as of emotion

8. The nomination committee decided to *block* the investigation of their decisions.
   a. to impede the passage of
   b. to support or strengthen
   c. to indicate broadly; sketch

Single Bar Graphs

Directions: This single bar graph shows the number of electoral votes for each of the 10 most-populated states. There are 538 electoral votes distributed among the 50 states and the District of Columbia. It takes 270 electoral votes to win an election. Use the information on the graph to answer the questions below.

1. How many electoral votes does California have? _____

2. How many electoral votes does Texas have? _____

3. What is the interval between numbers on the scale? _____

4. How many electoral votes does New Jersey have? _____

5. What is the difference in the number of votes between Michigan and Illinois?

   _____

6. Which state has exactly three fewer electoral votes than Texas?

   _____

7. What is the total number of electoral votes of the 10 most-populated states?

   _____

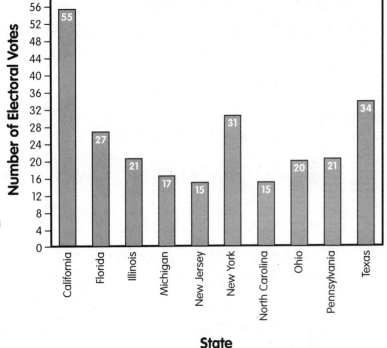

8. How many electoral votes are distributed among the remaining 40 states and the District of Columbia? _____

9. Why would a candidate spend more time campaigning in California than in North Carolina? _____

10. How many more votes in addition to these 10 states would be needed to win a presidential election? _____

Prepositions

Prepositions are words that show a relationship between other words.

To see how prepositions work, look at the words *fox* and *log*. Prepositions can show the relationship between the fox and the log:

The fox was *under* the log.　　　　The fox was *on* the log.

The fox was *by* the log.　　　　　The fox was *in* the log.

Prepositions always start prepositional phrases. A phrase is a group of words that doesn't make a whole sentence. The following are all prepositional phrases: *under the log, on the log, by the log, in the log.*

Part I

Directions: Write the prepositional phrase from each sentence on the line. Circle the object of the preposition and underline the preposition.

1. Penguins live at the South Pole.

_____

2. The students slept during the speech.

_____

3. The fish in the pan smelled awful.

_____

4. The announcer on TV was excited.

_____

5. I found the keys under the table.

_____

6. We are going to the movies tomorrow.

_____

7. The rabbit hopped across the road.

_____

8. The girls climbed to the top.

_____

Part II

Directions: Rewrite each sentence, adding a prepositional phrase to each.

1. The dog ate his dinner. The dog ate his dinner by the back door.

_____

2. The boys ran. _____

_____

3. Josh did his work. _____

_____

4. Sally is reading the book. _____

_____

Finding Median and Mode from Graphs

Math

Part I

Directions: Use the graph as your source for data. Then find the median (middle number) and mode (number that occurs most) for the set of data. Write your answers on the lines.

Fourth- and fifth-graders read books as part of their reading program. The number of books each class read in one week was totaled and graphed below.

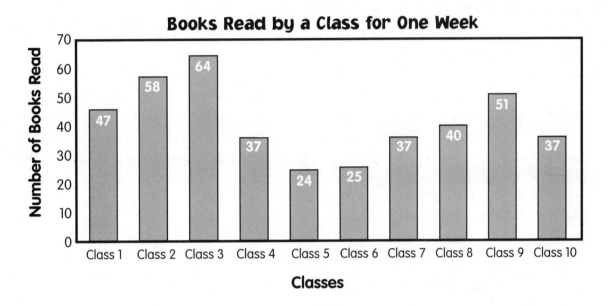

Books Read by a Class for One Week

1. What is the mode number of books read by the fourth- and fifth-grade classes? _____

2. What is the median number of books read by the fourth- and fifth-grade classes? _____

Part II

For each book read, students took a test. The results of their tests are seen below as percentages. *Hint:* To find the number of tests for each score, multiply the number of tests taken by the percentage.

1. Based on the percentages, if 100 tests were taken, how many students would score 60? _____

2. Based on the percentages, if 500 tests were taken, how many students would score 80 or 100? _____

3. What is the mode score? _____

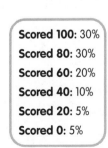

Scored **100:** 30%
Scored **80:** 30%
Scored **60:** 20%
Scored **40:** 10%
Scored **20:** 5%
Scored **0:** 5%

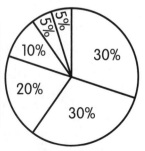

The Apology

Directions: This passage is an excerpt from the book *Do They Play Marbles on Mars?* by Margaret McAlister. Read the passage, and then answer the questions below.

"I saw that, Michael!" said Mrs. Jackson. "Come out here!"

"What?" I tried to look innocent. "What did I do?"

Mrs. Jackson sighed. She looked up at the ceiling then back at me.

"Apologize to Cheryl."

Now, that was really heavy. It was only a bit of crumpled paper. Nobody ever died from being hit on the head by an old math test.

Cheryl smirked. I glared at her. Cheryl had done much worse things to me. Mrs. Jackson hardly ever caught her. I should have just told Mrs. Jackson that Cheryl put a matchbox full of loose ants in my lunch box.

"Go ahead, Michael," said Mrs. Jackson. "Unless you'd like to pick up papers for a week."

I thought about it for a moment. It would almost be worth it to choose the papers, but then I thought of Cheryl following me around all week yelling insults while I picked up the trash. Then I would be forced to stuff some dirty, sticky wrappers down her T-shirt . . . and then I would get two weeks of picking up papers . . .

"Sorry," I muttered, looking at the floor.

1. Mrs. Jackson is most likely

    a. Cheryl's mother.   b. Michael's mother.   c. a teacher.   d. a cleaner.

2. Michael said he was sorry because

    a. Cheryl had been really hurt.   c. it was better than picking up papers.

    b. he hadn't meant to be nasty.   d. he had been in the wrong and knew it.

3. When Mrs. Jackson looked up at the ceiling, she was

    a. expecting something to fall from the ceiling.

    b. pretending to be bored by Michael's answer.

    c. wondering if she was about to get hit on the back of the head.

    d. having trouble with her eyes.

4. How well did Michael and Cheryl get along? Explain your answer. _____

_____

5. Why did Michael look at the floor when he apologized? _____

_____

6. The word "smirk" means to smile (happily   meanly   sweetly). (*Circle one.*)

Sports Table

Directions: Look at the chart below and answer the questions.

Children Aged 5–14 Years
Who Participated in Organized Sports Outside of School Hours
During the 12 Months Before April 2000

	Number			Participation Rate		
	Males	**Females**	**Total**	**Males**	**Females**	**Total**
Swimming	177,000	203,100	380,100	13.1%	15.8%	14.4%
Soccer (outdoor)	265,000	37,300	302,300	19.6%	2.9%	11.4%
Netball	6,400	234,900	241,300	0.5%	18.2%	9.1%
Tennis	124,800	99,100	223,900	9.2%	7.7%	8.5%
Basketball	119,600	80,700	200,300	8.8%	6.3%	7.6%
Australian-Rules Football	170,300	4,100	174,400	12.6%	0.3%	6.6%
Cricket (outdoor)	133,600	7,300	140,900	9.9%	0.6%	5.3%
Martial Arts	72,700	31,900	104,600	5.4%	2.5%	4.0%
Other Athletics	52,200	51,900	104,100	3.9%	4.0%	3.9%
Rugby League	92,500	2,500	95,000	6.8%	0.2%	3.6%

Source: Australian Bureau of Statistics, "Participation in the most popular sports," from *Year Book Australia 2003, Culture and Recreation: Children's Participation in Cultural and Leisure Activities.* Australia, April 2000, publication 4901.0. Data used with permission from the Australian Bureau of Statistics *(www.abs.gov.au).*

1. What sport was most played by boys in the 12 months before April 2000?_____

2. What percentage of boys played this sport?_____

3. What sport was most played by girls in the 12 months before April 2000? _____

4. What percentage of girls played this sport? _____

5. Did any girls play in the Rugby League? _____

6. Did any boys play Netball?_____

7. What sport had about the same number of boys and girls participating?_____

8. What does the figure 174,400 represent? _____

Putting It All Together

Directions: Use the following words to create 14 sentences. You can change the forms of the words (i.e., tense, singular to plural) as needed. Try to use one word from each list in each sentence. Try not to use any word twice.

Nouns	Verbs	Adjectives	Adverbs	Prepositions
scientist	shout	sad	quietly	into
squirrel	sniff	chilly	energetically	before
football	giggle	complicated	dismally	after
palm tree	consider	green	respectfully	until
asphalt	ski	enormous	yesterday	in
George	fly	miniscule	loudly	through
kangaroo	stare	sweet	happily	around
macaroni	shriek	confused	urgently	below
girl	dance	awkward	seriously	inside
ice cube	try	sleepy	encouragingly	during
broccoli	jump	pink	messily	under
sunflower	roar	silent	softly	on
Agnes	glare	filthy	despondently	over
cat	hop	sticky	sloppily	above

1. _____

2. _____

3. _____

4. _____

5. _____

6. _____

7. _____

8. _____

9. _____

10. _____

11. _____

12. _____

13. _____

14. _____

Potluck Dinner

Directions: The Potluck Dinner Club is held every Friday night at 6:30. Read the clues to find the time each member arrived, as well as the food item he or she brought. If the answer is "yes," make an **O** in the box. If the answer is "no," make an **X** in the box.

Clues

- ✿ Roland was late for the Potluck Dinner.
- ✿ Betty arrived after Charice.
- ✿ Paul arrived before the person who brought the spaghetti.
- ✿ Charice's rolls were still warm when she arrived.

- ✿ Heidi arrived right on time.
- ✿ Paul didn't bring the salad or the sodas.
- ✿ Betty brought the spaghetti, and Heidi brought the salad.
- ✿ Betty arrived at 6:15, and Paul arrived before Charice.

	5:45	6:00	6:15	6:30	6:45	Dessert	Rolls	Salad	Sodas	Spaghetti
Betty										
Charice										
Heidi										
Paul										
Roland										

1. Betty arrived at _____ and brought the _____.

2. Charice arrived at _____ and brought the _____.

3. Heidi arrived at _____ and brought the _____.

4. Paul arrived at _____ and brought the _____.

5. Roland arrived at _____ and brought the _____.

Droodles

Droodles are artistic interpretations of brainteasers. Pictures or illustrations are used to present information. Symbols may represent different things depending on the context. Word clues may be added.

Directions: What could these droodles be? Write your answers on the lines.

Droodle #1 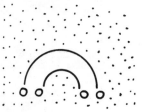 What could it be? _____ _____	**Droodle #2**  What could it be? _____ _____
Droodle #3  What could it be? _____ _____	**Droodle #4**  What could it be? _____ _____
Droodle #5 What could it be? _____ _____	**Droodle #6** 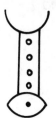 What could it be? _____ _____

Averages

Directions: Students in a sixth-grade classroom collected data by surveying classmates on a variety of subjects, including height, weight, grades, allowances, books read, and hours spent watching TV. Help them compute the average for each topic.

Reminder

To compute an average:

☼ Add all of the separate values in a set of data.

☼ Divide by the number of units of data.

☼ Round to the nearest integer.

---

1. A group of 9 boys in the classroom were measured for height. These were the heights recorded in inches: 51, 61, 57, 63, 60, 59, 60, 55, 62.

   Total: _____   Divided by: _____   Average: _____

2. A group of 11 students recorded these math scores: 88, 56, 92, 96, 100, 87, 66, 75, 81, 80, 90.

   Total: _____   Divided by: _____   Average: _____

3. These were the weights in pounds of 13 students surveyed: 88, 84, 77, 78, 90, 100, 106, 95, 96, 84, 88, 93, 81.

   Total: _____   Divided by: _____   Average: _____

4. A group of 10 students sold Valentine candy boxes during a school fund-raising project. These were the number of boxes sold: 14, 20, 12, 8, 6, 3, 15, 19, 24, 17.

   Total: _____   Divided by: _____   Average: _____

5. Thirteen students were surveyed on the number of hours they spent watching television in one week. These were the responses: 20, 23, 14, 7, 6, 1, 0, 15, 30, 20, 12, 8, 19.

   Total: _____   Divided by: _____   Average: _____

6. Sixteen students surveyed listed these weekly dollar allowances: 10, 9, 20, 0, 5, 1, 2, 8, 9, 5, 3, 0, 15, 14, 5, 3.

   Total: _____   Divided by: _____   Average: _____

Greek Mythology

Directions: Read the passage, and then answer the questions below using complete sentences.

The Myth of Narcissus

Zeus, the supreme god, persuaded Echo to distract his wife, Hera, by chattering incessantly. He did this so that Hera could not keep track of him, leaving him free to chase other women. However, when Hera figured out the plan, she was so enraged that she took away Echo's voice, leaving her with only the ability to repeat the final word of every message she heard. When Echo saw the extremely handsome but vain Narcissus, she fell deeply in love with him. Of course, she could not tell him of her love, but she followed him everywhere, gazing at him lovingly until he haughtily rejected her. Poor Echo hid in a cave and wasted away until only her voice remained. Then the goddess Nemesis decided to punish Narcissus by making him fall hopelessly in love with his own face as he saw it reflected in a pool. He gazed in fascination, unable to tear himself away from his image, until he gradually wasted away. In the spot where he had sat grew a beautiful yellow flower, which even to this day bears the name *narcissus*.

1. What did Zeus ask Echo to do? _____

   _____

2. Why did he ask her to do this? _____

   _____

3. What was Hera's reaction?_____

   _____

4. Why did Echo fall in love with Narcissus? _____

   _____

5. What was Narcissus's reaction to Echo? _____

   _____

6. What did Nemesis do to Narcissus? _____

   _____

7. What happened to Echo in the end? _____

   _____

8. What happened to Narcissus in the end? _____

   _____

Ratios

Directions: Discount Sporting Goods has thousands of items to appeal to every taste. Help the owners compute these ratios using the illustrations. The first one has been done for you.

Balls	⚾ ⚾ ⚾ ⚾ ⚾
Bats	🏏 🏏 🏏 🏏
Mitts	🥊 🥊
Shoes	👟 👟 👟

1. What is the ratio of baseballs to bats? ____5:4 or 5/4____

2. What is the ratio of bats to baseballs? _____

3. What is the ratio of mitts to balls? _____

4. What is the ratio of balls to mitts? _____

5. What is the ratio of shoes to balls? _____

6. What is the ratio of balls to shoes? _____

7. What is the ratio of bats to shoes? _____

8. What is the ratio of shoes to bats? _____

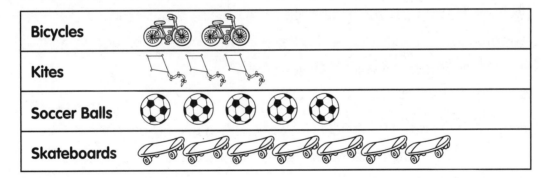

9. What is the ratio of bicycles to kites?_____

10. What is the ratio of kites to bicycles?_____

11. What is the ratio of skateboards to soccer balls?_____

12. What is the ratio of soccer balls to skateboards?_____

13. What is the ratio of kites to skateboards?_____

14. What is the ratio of skateboards to kites?_____

Sentence Combining

Directions: Read both sentences. Circle the answer that shows the best way in which to combine them to make one sentence.

> ### Example
> 1. The flag is red, white, and blue. The flag has fifty stars.
>   a. The red, white, and blue flag 50 stars has.
>   b. Fifty stars the red, white, and blue flag has.
>   (c.) The red, white, and blue flag has fifty stars.

1. The dog is black. The dog has white patches.
    a. The dog is black, and the dog has white patches.
    b. The dog is black and has white patches.
    c. White patches the black dog has.

2. It is hot today. It is humid today.
    a. It is hot and humid today.
    b. Hot and humid it is today.
    c. Today, it is hot and it is humid.

3. Jason won the foot race. Jason hurt his leg while winning the foot race.
    a. Jason won the foot race and hurt his leg while winning the foot race.
    b. The foot race Jason won while hurting his leg.
    c. Jason won the foot race but hurt his leg.

4. Yesterday, I went to the mall. I bought two books and a pair of sandals.
    a. Yesterday, I went to the mall and bought two books and a pair of sandals.
    b. Two books and a pair of sandals I bought at the mall yesterday.
    c. At the mall yesterday, I went and bought two books and a pair of sandals.

5. I have to study for my social studies test. I have to do ten math problems.
    a. Ten math problems and study for my social studies test I have to.
    b. I have to study for my social studies test, and then I have to do ten math problems.
    c. I have to study for my social studies test and do ten math problems.

Rate Problems

Directions: Compute the rate in each of the problems below.

> ### Reminders
> ☼ To determine the rate of speed, divide the distance traveled by the time it took to travel that distance.
> ☼ The formula is: $r = \dfrac{d}{t}$
> ☼ The answer is usually expressed in miles per hour (m.p.h.).

1. Your family took a 360-mile automobile trip from Los Angeles to San Francisco in 6 hours. What was your average speed in miles per hour? _____ m.p.h.

2. The Clark family drove 3,000 miles from New York to Los Angeles in 60 hours. What was their average rate? _____ m.p.h.

3. The Brown family traveled 990 miles from Atlanta, Georgia, to Houston, Texas, in 33 hours. What was their average rate of speed? _____ m.p.h.

4. Mark's mother drove 2,340 miles from Cincinnati, Ohio, to Portland, Oregon, in 39 hours. What was her average rate of speed? _____ m.p.h.

5. Shannon's father drove 2,750 miles from Seattle, Washington, to Philadelphia, Pennsylvania, in 55 hours. What was his average speed in miles per hour? _____ m.p.h.

6. Michelle's family drove 2,200 miles from Houston, Texas, to Portland, Oregon, in 40 hours. What was their average rate of speed? _____ m.p.h.

7. Alyssa's family drove 3,060 miles from San Francisco, California, to Boston, Massachusetts, in 60 hours. What was their average speed? _____ m.p.h.

8. Frank's dad drove 1,600 miles from Minneapolis, Minnesota, to Seattle, Washington, in 40 hours. What was his average speed in miles per hour? _____ m.p.h.

9. Stacy's mother drove 1,040 miles from Denver, Colorado, to Memphis, Tennessee, in 26 hours. What was her average speed? _____ m.p.h.

10. Jake's dad flew a plane 200 miles from Kansas City, Missouri, to Omaha, Nebraska, in 2.5 hours. What was the plane's average speed? _____ m.p.h.

Poetry About Me

Part I

Directions: Phrase poetry can describe an item or person without using complete sentences. Write a phrase poem using the example poem as a guide. End your phrase poem with a word that describes the subject of the poem.

Morgan
rides a bike
loves spaghetti
chats on the phone
kicks the soccer ball
loves babies
Alive!

Subject: _____

Phrase 1: _____

Phrase 2: _____

Phrase 3: _____

Phrase 4: _____

Phrase 5: _____

One Word: _____

Part II

Directions: Fill in the blanks below and you will have a poem about the person you know best—you!

I am _____

And _____

But I am not _____

Or _____

I like _____

And _____

But I don't like _____

Or _____

I feel _____

But I don't feel _____

Finding the Rate

Directions: *Rate* tells the measure of one quantity as it relates to the value of another quantity. Find the rate. Round to the nearest hundredth if your answer is not an integer. The first one has been done for you.

1. Bill can walk 3 miles in 45 minutes. How long will it take Bill to walk 10 miles? $$\frac{1 \quad \cancel{3} \text{ miles}}{15 \quad \cancel{45} \text{ min.}} = \frac{10 \text{ miles}}{n}$$ It will take Bill __150__ minutes.	2. Marcie can jog a mile every 6 minutes. How many miles can Marcie jog in 30 minutes? Marcie can jog _____ miles.
3. Andrew can skate 1 block every 15 seconds. How many blocks can Andrew skate in 2 minutes? Andrew can skate _____ blocks.	4. Mona drove 40 miles per hour. How long will it take Mona to drive 100 miles? It will take Mona _____ hours.
5. The airplane flies 725 miles per hour. How many minutes will it take the plane to fly 150 miles? It will take the plane _____ minutes.	6. It takes Olivia 30 seconds to count to 25. How many minutes will it take Olivia to count to 300? It will take Olivia _____ minutes.

It's Nonsense!

Directions: "Jabberwocky," a poem of nonsense verse, was originally featured in the book *Through the Looking Glass, and What Alice Found There* by Lewis Carroll. Read the poem, and then answer the questions below.

Jabberwocky

by Lewis Carroll

'Twas brillig, and the slithy toves
Did gyre and gimble in the wabe:
All mimsy were the borogoves,
And the mome raths outgrabe.

"Beware the Jabberwock, my son!
The jaws that bite, the claws that catch!
Beware the Jubjub bird, and shun
The frumious Bandersnatch!"

He took his vorpal sword in hand:
Long time the manxome foe he sought—
So rested he by the Tumtum tree,
And stood awhile in thought.

And, as in uffish thought he stood,
The Jabberwock, with eyes of flame,

Came whiffling through the tulgey wood,
And burbled as it came!

One, two! One, two! And through and through
The vorpal blade went snicker-snack!
He left it dead, and with its head
He went galumphing back.

"And hast thou slain the Jabberwock?
Come to my arms, my beamish boy!
O frabjous day! Callooh! Callay!"
He chortled in his joy.

'Twas brillig, and the slithy toves
Did gyre and gimble in the wabe:
All mimsy were the borogoves,
And the mome raths outgrabe.

1. What did the slithy toves do in the wabe?

   a. outgrabe

   b. gyre and gimble

   c. mimsy

   d. snicker-snack

2. What is a Jabberwock?

   a. a kind of fairy

   b. a kind of monster

   c. a kind of wizard

   d. none of these

3. What kind of sound did the vorpol blade make?

   a. burble

   b. Callooh

   c. snicker-snack

   d. Callay

4. How does the poet describe the Bandersnatch?

   a. mimsy

   b. tulgey

   c. uffish

   d. frumious

Crossword Challenge

Directions: Put the words below into the crossword puzzle. Make sure that each word touches at least one other word.

> **Monday**   **Thursday**   **Saturday**
>
> **Wednesday**   **Friday**   **Sunday**

					T	U	E	S	D	A	Y

Find the Snakes

Directions: Look for "snakes" that equal twenty-four. The numbers have to be touching. (You cannot jump around.) Once you find them, circle them. *Note:* You may use a number more than once.

Example

5	+	7	+
+	8	+	12
7	+	4	+
+	9	+	6

2	+	5	×	2	+	8	×	4	÷
+	10	+	5	+	6	–	2	÷	2
5	×	3	×	2	+	6	+	5	+
×	2	+	7	+	1	×	4	×	8
3	×	12	+	2	×	2	×	3	×
+	15	–	5	÷	6	–	16	–	5
5	×	3	×	14	+	10	÷	11	–
×	6	–	1	–	6	×	4	+	4
7	–	4	+	7	+	12	+	6	×
+	11	×	2	–	16	+	15	–	4

All About Me

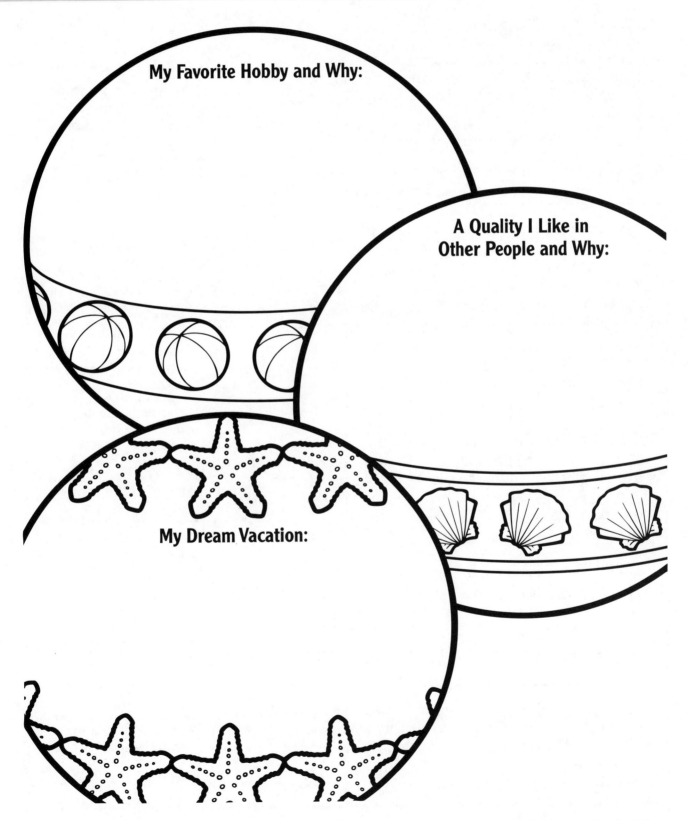

My Favorite Hobby and Why:

A Quality I Like in
Other People and Why:

My Dream Vacation:

Summer Reading List

☼ **Before We Were Free** by Julia Alvarez

Anita must hide with her family in the Dominican Republic during the 1960s. She is an average twelve-year-old adolescent. She keeps a secret diary where she discusses her situation, as well as her obsession with boys and her appearance.

Themes: family ties, courage, the cost of freedom

☼ **The Fighting Ground** by Avi

The popular children's author tells the tale of Jonathan, a thirteen year old who fights in the Revolutionary War. The boy soon finds that the real battle is within himself.

Themes: facing fear, humanity, values

☼ **The Penderwicks: A Summer Tale of Four Sisters, Two Rabbits, and a Very Interesting Boy** by Jeanne Birdsall

Four sisters and their father spend the summer in the Berkshire Mountains. There, they share adventures with a local boy. This is a heartwarming tale of a loving family. It received the National Book Award in 2005.

Themes: family loyalty, typical childhood behaviors, resilience

☼ **George Washington Carver** by Tonya Bolden

This is the amazing-but-true story of a man who was born a slave and became a conservationist, scientist, researcher, and teacher. It includes photos and reproductions of Carver's own paintings.

Themes: adversity, fortitude, inventing

☼ **Jim Thorpe's Bright Path** by Joseph Bruchac

Jim Thorpe was the greatest American Indian athlete. This book focuses on how his boyhood set the stage for his international fame.

Themes: importance of hard work, tenacity, competition

☼ **Sahara Special** by Esmé Raji Codell

Sahara is struggling with school and her feelings caused by her father's leaving. She gets a new start with a special teacher who supports her writing talents, as well as her individuality.

Themes: uniqueness, inner strength, hope

Making the Most of Summertime Reading

When reading these books, ask yourself the questions below. Answering these questions will enhance and improve your reading comprehension skills.

☼ Why did you choose this book to read?

☼ Name a character from the story that you like. Why do you like him or her?

☼ Where does the story take place? Do you want to vacation there?

☼ Name a problem that occurs in the story. How is it resolved?

☼ What is the best part of the story so far? Describe it!

☼ What do you think is going to happen next in the story? Make a prediction!

☼ Who are the important characters in the story? Why are they important?

☼ What is the book about?

☼ What are two things you have learned by reading this book?

☼ Would you tell your friend to read this book? Why or why not?

Summer Reading List

✿ **Waiting for Normal** by Leslie Connor

Addie is looking for a normal life while living with her irresponsible mother in a trailer in upstate New York. This book has humor, tension, and well-developed characters.

Themes: looking for the positive, dysfunctional parent, endurance

✿ **Solving Zoe** by Barbara Dee

This is a mystery—where the reader uses clues to unlock the codes and ciphers that Zoe and Lucas, who are students at a private school, try to figure out.

Themes: friendship, feelings of inferiority, wanting to belong

✿ **My Last Skirt: The Story of Jennie Hodgers, Union Soldier** by Lynda Durrant

Jennie is a poor Irish immigrant who disguises herself as a boy and enlists in the Union Army during the Civil War.

Themes: bravery, survival, understanding oneself

✿ **Operation Redwood** by S. Terrell French

Julian Carter-Li and his friends fight to save a grove of redwood trees in northern California.

Themes: ecology, working together, fighting the establishment

✿ **Diamond Willow** by Helen Frost

Willow, a twelve-year-old Alaskan girl, sets out to take her wounded dog to her grandparents' house. But during her journey, they get caught in a blizzard, and Willow must make difficult decisions. This is told in diamond-shaped, easy-to-read verse.

Themes: connection to the past, overcoming adversity, respect for nature

✿ **Deep and Dark and Dangerous: A Ghost Story** by Mary Downing Hahn

When thirteen-year-old Ali spends the summer with her aunt and cousin at the family's vacation home, she discovers a secret that her mother has been hiding for over thirty years.

Themes: identity, overcoming fear, understanding the truth

✿ **Scat** by Carl Hiaasen

Nick and Marta must find out what happened to the biology teacher after she disappears on a school field trip to a swamp. This is an eco-mystery set in Florida.

Themes: ecology, positive outlook, overcoming grief

✿ **Any Small Goodness: A Novel of the Barrio** by Tony Johnston

Arturo and his family leave Mexico for East Los Angeles. Short vignettes (chapters) make this a good choice for reading aloud.

Themes: family relationships, cultural differences, coping with difficulties

Summer Reading List
(cont.)

☼ **Day of Tears** by Julius Lester

This is a historical novel about the largest slave auction in United States history. It is told in dialogue and through monologues and may be best read aloud with an adult, as difficult conversations may ensue. It received the Corretta Scott King Award.

Themes: slavery, inhumanity, injustice

☼ **Odysseus** (retold) by Geraldine McCaughrean

Odysseus journeys home after years of fighting in the Trojan War. He and his men encounter monsters, are imprisoned, and fight battles with nature as they attempt to return to Ithaca. This book is filled with violent events and gory details.

Themes: loyalty, hardship, triumph

☼ **Miss Spitfire: Reaching Helen Keller** by Sarah Miller

This is the oft-told tale of Annie Sullivan and her challenge and determination to teach the blind and deaf Helen Keller. In this version, it is told from the point of view of Sullivan, which makes for an especially uplifting conclusion.

Themes: never giving up, aspiration, inspiration

☼ **Sixth-Grade Glommers, Norks, and Me** by Lisa Papademetriou

This hilarious book describes Allie, who is starting middle school and is intimidated about going to a special school away from her neighborhood.

Themes: finding your way, individualism, pride

☼ **Canned** by Alex Shearer

Fergal Bamfield has a rather interesting hobby—he collects tin cans. When he meets Charlotte, a fellow can collector, the two come upon cans with gruesome things inside. Despite the gory subject matter, this wacky novel is very funny. It is set in England and contains some English jargon.

Themes: misfits, friendship, working out problems

☼ **Maniac Magee** by Jerry Spinelli

This Newbery-Award-winning book chronicles a resourceful orphan who must make his own way in the world after running away from an impossible living situation.

Themes: race relationships, making the best of bad situations, hope

☼ **When You Reach Me** by Rebecca Stead

Miranda has her world turned upside-down when she receives some future-predicting notes. Contemporary New York City is the setting for this mystery.

Themes: friendship, family, identity

☼ **100 Cupboards** by N. D. Wilson

Twelve-year-old Henry York is sent to live with his aunt and uncle after his parents are kidnapped in South America. Soon after arriving, he finds that there is something strange in the wall behind his bed. This novel is funny, suspenseful, and gory. It is meant for the more mature reader.

Themes: evil, overcoming obstacles, working together

Fun Ways to Love Books

Here are some fun ways that your child can expand on his or her reading. Some of these ideas will involve both you and your child; however, the wording has been directed towards your child because we want him or her to be inspired to love books.

Write to the Author

Many authors love to hear from their readers, especially when they hear what people liked best about their books. You can write to an author and send your letter in care of the book's publisher. The publisher's address is listed directly after the title page. Or you may go to the author's Web site and follow the directions for how to send the author a letter. (To make sure your author is still living, do a search on the Internet by typing the author's name into a search engine.)

A Comic Book

Turn your favorite book into a comic book. Fold at least two sheets of paper in half, and staple them so they make a book. With a ruler and pencil, draw boxes across each page to look like blank comic strips. Then draw the story of your book as if it were a comic. Draw pictures of your characters, and have words coming out of their mouths—just as in a real comic strip.

Always Take a Book

Maybe you've had to wait with your parents in line at the post office or in the vet's waiting room with nothing to do. If you get into the habit of bringing a book with you wherever you go, you'll always have something exciting to do! Train yourself to always take a good book. You might want to carry a small backpack or shoulder bag—something that allows you to carry a book easily from place to place. Don't forget a bookmark!

Novel Foods

What foods do the characters in your book eat? What do they drink? What are their favorite foods? Get a better sense of your character's tastes by cooking their favorite foods. Some characters love sweet things, like cookies and ice cream. Other characters like hamburgers and pizza. Decide what foods your characters love. Locate appropriate recipes on the Internet or in books. Then make up a grocery list. Buy groceries and gather necessary materials, such as mixing bowls, spoons, and pans. Cook your characters' favorite foods by yourself or with friends.

Write a Sequel

What happens to the characters in your book after you finish reading the final page? Why not create a sequel? A sequel is a book that is published after the first book has enjoyed success among readers. Sequels generally pick up where the first book left off. For example, the sequel to Madeleine L'Engle's novel *A Wrinkle in Time* is *A Wind in the Door.*

Bookmark Your Words

Make summertime reading lots of fun with these reading log glasses. Have your child fill in the glasses after his or her daily reading. Once your child has completed the glasses, he or she can cut them out and use them as bookmarks.

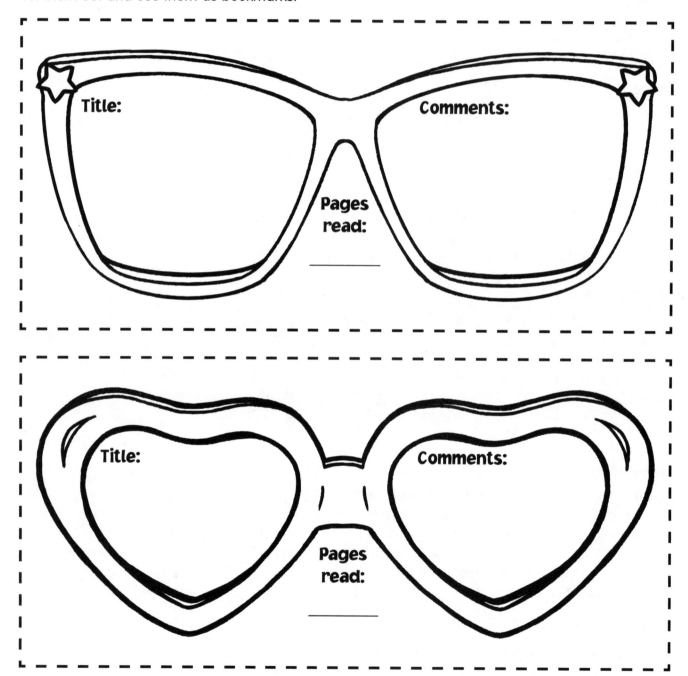

This page may be reproduced as many times as needed.

Read-Together Chart

Do you read books to your sibling(s) before bed? Perhaps your mother reads to the family at breakfast? You may enjoy sharing a book with a friend while waiting for the bus. You and your family and friends can create a Read-Together Chart and fill it in to keep track of all the books you've read together.

Here are two Read-Together Charts. The first one is a sample. The second one has been left blank, so you can add your own categories and books.

Sample Chart

Book We Read	Who Read It?	Summary	Our Review
The Secret Garden	My older sister read it to me.	It's about a spoiled girl who learns to love nature and people.	We like this book. The characters are funny, and the illustrations are beautiful!

Your Chart

This page may be reproduced as many times as needed.

Journal Topics

Choose one of these journal topics each day. Make sure you add enough detail so someone else reading it will clearly be able to know at least four of the following:

> ☼ **who**　☼ **what**　☼ **when**　☼ **where**　☼ **why**　☼ **how**

1. The best sport or game to play with my friends is . . .
2. If I had a pen pal in Australia or India (or another country), I would ask him or her . . .
3. If I could get a job after school, I would like to . . .
4. If I had to choose being caught in an earthquake, tornado, or flood, I would pick . . .
5. One resolution I would like to keep for next year is . . .
6. If I were on a committee to pick the best snack food in the world, I'd choose . . .
7. One of the activities I do well and could explain to someone else is . . .
8. I would (or would not) like to be a doctor because . . .
9. If I were going to interview the president of the United States or the leader of another country, the one question I would be sure to ask is . . .
10. The type of music I most enjoy is . . .
11. Thinking about the behavior of the students at my school, I feel . . .
12. If I were on a committee to improve health and reduce the amount of obesity in children, I would suggest . . .
13. I think (or don't think) parents should be able to choose a specific teacher for their child because . . .
14. Since scientists say global warming is such a problem, my opinion is that we should . . .
15. Students should (or should not) be able to bring their cell phones to school because . . .
16. It is easy to get a pizza delivered to a home. One item that cannot be delivered but should be is . . .
17. I would rather travel by plane (car, bus, or train) because . . .
18. One item I have bought with my own money is . . .
19. My favorite aunt (uncle, or cousin) is . . .
20. The perfect way to eat ice cream is . . .
21. My favorite pet (or the pet I would like to have) is . . .
22. If I could own a business when I grow up, it would be . . .
23. If I went on vacation and could choose to stay in a hotel or go camping, I would . . .
24. If I could build my own house anywhere I wanted, the kind of community I would choose would be . . .
25. One great thing about a rainy day is . . .

Learning Experiences

Here are some fun, low-cost activities that you can do with your child. You'll soon discover that these activities can be stimulating, educational, and complementary to the other exercises in this book.

Flash Cards

Make up all types of flash cards. Depending on your child's interest and grade level, these cards might feature enrichment words, math problems, or states and capitals. You can create them yourself with markers or on a computer. Let your child help cut pictures out of magazines and glue them on. Then find a spot outdoors and go through the flash cards with your child.

Project Pantry

Find a spot in your house where you can store supplies. This might be a closet or a bin that stays in one spot. Get some clean paint cans or buckets. Fill them with all types of craft and art supplies. Besides the typical paints, markers, paper, scissors, and glue, include some more unusual things, such as tiles, artificial flowers, and wrapping paper. This way, whenever you and your child want to do a craft project, you have everything you need at that moment.

Collect Something

Let your child choose something to collect that is free or inexpensive, such as paper clips or buttons. If your child wants to collect something that might be impractical, like horses, find pictures in magazines or catalogs, and have your child cut them out and start a picture collection.

How Much Does It Cost?

If you go out for a meal, have your child help total the bill. Write down the cost of each person's meal. Then add it all together. You can vary this and make it much simpler by having your child just figure out the cost of an entrée and a drink or the cost of three desserts. You might want to round the figures.

Nature Scavenger Hunt

Take a walk, go to a park, or hike in the mountains. But before you go, create a scavenger hunt list for your child. This can consist of all sorts of things found in nature. Make sure he or she has a bag to carry everything that is found. (Be sure to check ahead of time about the rules or laws regarding removing anything.) You might include things like a leaf with pointed edges, a speckled rock, and a twig with two small limbs on it. Take a few minutes to look at all the things your child has collected, and check them off the list.

Take a Trip, and Keep a Journal

If you are going away during the summer, have your child keep a journal. Depending upon his or her preference, this journal can take a different look. One option is for your child to collect postcards and paste them into a blank journal. He or she can also draw pictures of the places he or she is visiting. Another option is for your child to keep a traditional journal and draw pictures. Your child can also do a photo-journal if a camera is available for him or her to use.

Web Sites

Math Web Sites

☼ **AAA Math:** http://www.aaamath.com/
This site contains hundreds of pages of basic math skills divided by grade or topic.

☼ **AllMath.com:** http://www.allmath.com/
This site has math flashcards, biographies of mathematicians, and a math glossary.

☼ **BrainBashers:** http://www.brainbashers.com/
This is a unique collection of brainteasers, games, and optical illusions.

☼ **Coolmath.com:** http://www.coolmath.com/
Explore this amusement park of mathematics! Have fun with the interactive activities.

☼ **Mrs. Glosser's Math Goodies:** http://www.mathgoodies.com/
This is a free, educational Web site featuring interactive worksheets, puzzles, and more!

Reading and Writing Web Sites

☼ **Aesop's Fables:** http://www.umass.edu/aesop/
This site has almost forty of the fables. Both traditional and modern versions are presented.

☼ **American Library Association:** http://ala.org/
Visit this site to find out both the past and present John Newbery Medal and Randolph Caldecott Medal winners.

☼ **Book Adventure:** http://www.bookadventure.com/
This site features a free reading incentive program dedicated to encouraging children in grades K–8 to read.

☼ **Chateau Meddybemps—Young Writers Workshop:** http://www.meddybemps.com/9.700
Use the provided story starters to help your child write a story.

☼ **Fairy Godmother:** http://www.fairygodmother.com/
This site will capture your child's imagination and spur it on to wonderful creativity.

☼ **Grammar Gorillas:** http://www.funbrain.com/grammar/
Play grammar games on this site that proves that grammar can be fun!

☼ **Graphic Organizers:** http://www.eduplace.com/graphicorganizer/
Use these graphic organizers to help your child write in an organized manner.

☼ **Rhymezone:** http://www.rhymezone.com/
Type in the word you want to rhyme. If there is a rhyming word to match your word, you'll find it here.

Web Sites (cont.)

Reading and Writing Web Sites (cont.)

☼ **Storybook:** http://www.kids-space.org/story/story.html

Storybook has published children's stories on this Web site. Just like in a library, children can choose a shelf and read stories.

☼ **Wacky Web Tales:** http://www.eduplace.com/tales/index.html

This is a great place for budding writers to submit their stories and read other children's writing.

☼ **Write on Reader:** http://library.thinkquest.org/J001156/

Children can visit Write on Reader to gain a love of reading and writing.

General Web Sites

☼ **Animal Photos:** http://nationalzoo.si.edu/

This site offers wonderful pictures of animals, as well as virtual zoo visits.

☼ **Animal Planet:** http://animal.discovery.com/

Best for older kids, children can watch videos or play games at this site for animal lovers.

☼ **Congress for Kids:** http://www.congressforkids.net/index.htm

Children can go to this site to learn all about the branches of the United States Government.

☼ **Dinosaur Guide:** http://dsc.discovery.com/dinosaurs/

This is an interactive site on dinosaurs that goes beyond just learning about the creatures.

☼ **The Dinosauria:** http://www.ucmp.berkeley.edu/diapsids/dinosaur.html

This site focuses on dispelling dinosaur myths. Read about fossils, history, and more.

☼ **Earthquake Legends:** http://www.fema.gov/kids/eqlegnd

On this site, children can read some of the tales behind earthquakes that people of various cultures once believed.

☼ **The Electronic Zoo:** http://netvet.wustl.edu/e-zoo.htm

This site has links to thousands of animal sites covering every creature under the sun!

☼ **Great Buildings Online:** http://www.greatbuildings.com/

This gateway to architecture around the world and across history documents a thousand buildings and hundreds of leading architects.

☼ **Maggie's Earth Adventure:** http://www.missmaggie.org/

Join Maggie and her dog, Dude, on a wonderful Earth adventure.

☼ **Mr. Dowling's Electronic Passport:** http://www.mrdowling.com/index.html

This is an incredible history and geography site.

☼ **Tropical Twisters:** http://kids.earth.nasa.gov/archive/hurricane/index.html

Take an in-depth look at hurricanes, from how they're created to how dangerous they are.

Commonly Misspelled Words

Here are some of the most commonly misspelled words in the English language. Use this list to help you spell the words correctly.

accept	humor	recommend
advice	independent	rhyme
believe	intelligence	rhythm
calendar	judgment	scary
changeable	length	sentence
choose	library	separate
collectible	lose	similar
conscience	miniature	success
definitely	mischievous	temperature
dictionary	misspell	tomorrow
easily	naturally	tries
embarrass	necessary	truly
exceed	noticeable	twelfth
excellence	occasionally	unique
experience	opinion	until
explanation	opportunity	usually
fascinating	personal	vacuum
February	piece	valuable
finally	possession	visible
foreign	prejudice	weather
grateful	privilege	Wednesday
happily	realize	weird
height	really	writing
heroes	receive	young

Proofreading Marks

Editor's Mark	Meaning	Example
≡	capitalize	they fished in lake tahoe.
/	make it lowercase	Five Students missed the Bus.
sp.	spelling mistake	The day was clowdy and cold. _(sp.)_
⊙	add a period	Tomorrow is a holiday⊙
ℓ	delete (remove)	One person knew the the answer.
∧	add a word	Six ∧ were in the litter. _(pups)_
∧̦	add a comma	He planted peaș corn, and squash.
∼	reverse words or letters	An otter swam in the bed kelp.
∨	add an apostrophe	The child's bike was blue.
⌄⌄ ⌄⌄	add quotation marks	Why can't I go? she cried.
#	make a space	He ate two red# apples.
⌒	close the space	Her favorite game is soft ball.
⁋	begin a new paragraph	to know. ⁋ Next on the list

Multiplication Chart

X	0	1	2	3	4	5	6	7	8	9	10	11	12
0	0	0	0	0	0	0	0	0	0	0	0	0	0
1	0	1	2	3	4	5	6	7	8	9	10	11	12
2	0	2	4	6	8	10	12	14	16	18	20	22	24
3	0	3	6	9	12	15	18	21	24	27	30	33	36
4	0	4	8	12	16	20	24	28	32	36	40	44	48
5	0	5	10	15	20	25	30	35	40	45	50	55	60
6	0	6	12	18	24	30	36	42	48	54	60	66	72
7	0	7	14	21	28	35	42	49	56	63	70	77	84
8	0	8	16	24	32	40	48	56	64	72	80	88	96
9	0	9	18	27	36	45	54	63	72	81	90	99	108
10	0	10	20	30	40	50	60	70	80	90	100	110	120
11	0	11	22	33	44	55	66	77	88	99	110	121	132
12	0	12	24	36	48	60	72	84	96	108	120	132	144

Measurement Tools

Measurement Conversion Chart

![cup]	cups (c.)	1	2	4	8	16
![milk carton]	pints (pt.)	$\frac{1}{2}$	1	2	4	8
![milk]	quarts (qt.)	$\frac{1}{4}$	$\frac{1}{2}$	1	2	4
![gallon]	gallons (gal.)	$\frac{1}{16}$	$\frac{1}{8}$	$\frac{1}{4}$	$\frac{1}{2}$	1

Inch Ruler Cutout

Directions: Cut out the two ruler parts, and tape them together.

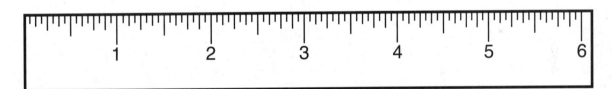

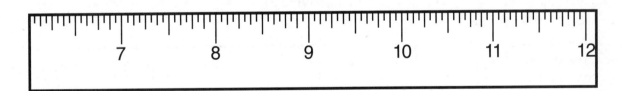

Centimeter Ruler Cutout

Answer Key

Page 11

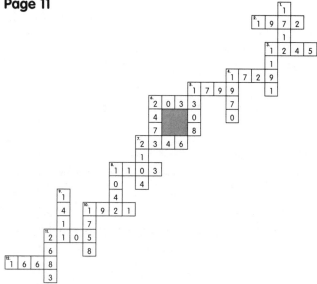

Page 12

1. b   2. b   3. c   4. a

Page 13

2. 2,516
3. 986
4. 642,873
5. 32,824
6. 21,033
7. 2,277
8. 109,272
9. 3,634,770
10. 43,183
11. 19,241
12. 950,544

Page 14

Answers will vary.

Page 15

2. 41,916 ÷ 28 = 1,497
   Check: 1,497 x 28 = 41,916
3. 33,320 ÷ 136 = 245
   Check: 245 x 136 = 33,320
4. 3,600 ÷ 90 = 40
   Check: 40 x 90 = 3,600
5. 8,928 ÷ 9 = 992
   Check: 992 x 9 = 8,928
6. 28,917 ÷ 81 = 357
   Check: 357 x 81 = 28,917
7. 35,620 ÷ 260 = 137
   Check: 137 x 260 = 35,620
8. 180,930 ÷ 37 = 4,890
   Check: 4,890 x 37 = 180,930
9. 8,840 ÷ 65 = 136
   Check: 136 x 65 = 8,840

Page 16

1. a   2. b   3. d   4. a

Page 17

1. $93.96
2. $4.47
3. $105.30
4. $69.93
5. $53.38
6. $420.52
7. $585.39
8. $256.50
9. 2.646
10. 1.872
11. 2.6628
12. 0.00228
13. $6.30
14. 4.78
15. 137.74
16. $1.38
17. $8.37
18. 0.1218

Page 18

2. egg
3. time
4. cream
5. bomb
6. bag
7. flash
8. cart
9. light
10. hall
11. apple
12. pen
13. horse
14. love
15. eye

Page 19

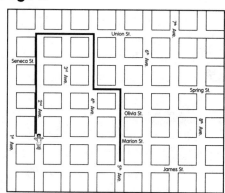

Page 20

2. caribou
3. okapi or ant
4. llama
5. monkey(s)
6. mouse
7. frog
8. rat
9. fox
10. hen

Page 21

Answer Key (cont.)

Page 22

Page 23

Part I

1. 15 minutes/900 seconds
2. 30 minutes/1,800 seconds
3. 45 minutes/2,700 seconds
4. 60 minutes/3,600 seconds
5. 120 minutes/7,200 seconds
6. 180 minutes/10,800 seconds
7. 240 minutes/14,400 seconds
8. 360 minutes/21,600 seconds
9. 480 minutes/28,800 seconds
10. 720 minutes/43,200 seconds
11. 1,080 minutes/64,800 seconds
12. 1,440 minutes/86,400 seconds

Part II

1. >   2. <   3. >   4. >

Page 24

1. a   2. c   3. b   4. c

Page 25

Page 26

Answers will vary, but words may be used in the following ways:

1. Avery's *fast* lasted six days. (n)
   My new watch is *fast*. (adj)
2. Corinne stood by her friend's *side*. (n)
   The thief left using the *side* door. (adj)
3. Which *number* did you draw? (n)
   Number your paper one through six. (v)
4. Get a *good* night's sleep before the test. (adj)
   The peddler sold his *goods* from a truck. (n)
5. Our lawyer thinks we have a *just* cause. (adj)
   That cake has *just* enough chocolate in it. (adv)
6. Our captain ordered a *retreat* from the field. (n)
   "*Retreat!*" yelled our captain. (v)

Page 27

1. 467.476 mi.   6. 44.636 mi.
2. 2,246.8 mi.   7. 177.813 m.p.h.
3. 32.422 ft.   8. 3,030.957 lbs.
4. 94.14 mi.   9. 91.05 mi.
5. 15.23 mi.   10. 880.431 mi.

Page 28

1. a   2. c   3. b   4. c

Page 29

	Monday	Tuesday	Wednesday	Thursday	Art Exhibit	Fair	Movie Premiere	Sporting Event
Ana	O	X	X	X	X	O	X	X
Dave	X	O	X	X	X	X	O	X
Maria	X	X	O	X	X	X	X	O
Steve	X	X	X	O	O	X	X	X

1. Ana went to the _____fair_____ on _____Monday_____ .
2. Dave went to the _____movie premiere_____ on _____Tuesday_____ .
3. Maria went to the _____sporting event_____ on _____Thursday_____ .
4. Steve went to the _____art exhibit_____ on _____Wednesday_____ .

Page 30

1. Nets   5. Eagles   9. Jazz
2. Padres   6. Lions   10. Kings
3. Mets   7. Pistons   11. Clippers
4. Colts   8. Marlins   12. Braves

Answer Key *(cont.)*

Page 31

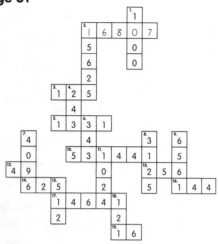

Page 32

The main idea is *b*.

1. A great monster leaped from the shadows and blocked their way.
2. The ugly beast had purple eyes.
3. Above them, a horn rose from the center of its forehead.
4. Its bright orange skin showed beneath a thin layer of coarse, black hair.
5. It reached its claws toward the terrified group.
6. It snarled menacingly, revealing a mouthful of sharp teeth.

Page 33

H. 2	X. -21	C. 13
Q. -4	S. -1	N. 1
D. -2	A. -9	M. 12
B. -18	V. 6	I. -5
F. 0	U. 11	P. 22
G. -11	E. -16	T. 3
O. -3	Y. 5	R. -20
W. -15	J. -21	L. -41
K. -6	Z. 8	

Riddle: He thought he would be a good drill sergeant.

Page 34

Answers will vary.

Page 35

1. $1	4. 7	7. $6	10. -72
2. $1	5. $21	8. -24	11. -32
3. $11	6. 2	9. 17	12. $226

Page 36

1. ABN	3. no	5. repeat
2. 1 hour	4. ABN	6. 3

7. *Night Train, Stage Divers,* or Movie: *Ozone*
8. False
9. False
10. True
11. *Pet Hotline*
12. *Pacific Post*
13. Saturday, January 22
14. *Holiday Line*

Page 37

1. $12	4. $7	7. $270	10. 5
2. $20	5. -9	8. 156	11. $5
3. 42	6. 10	9. -64	12. 20

Page 38

Answers will vary.

Page 39

2	9	12		5	13	10		6		2	14		9
			2				3		5				1
14						11		1	12			4	6
4	11	14	8	6	10	13	9			6	9		
12	1	2	12	6	5		10	6		14		2	9
8	4	14	9	13	3		5	8	7	5	12	7	
14	2	8	11	3	10		1	4	11	9	14	1	

Page 40

1. Patriots
2. Twins
3. Timberwolves
4. Avalanche
5. Saints
6. Dodgers
7. Sharks
8. Bears
9. Bulls
10. Lightning
11. A's
12. 49ers

Page 41

2. 30	7. 6	12. 36
3. 25	8. 18	13. 8
4. 1	9. 0	14. 5
5. 63	10. 20	15. 18
6. 53	11. 86	

Answer Key *(cont.)*

Page 42
Answers will vary.

Page 43

1. 130 yds.
2. 260 cm
3. 330 ft.
4. 630 m
5. 250 cm
6. 722 mm
7. 221 m
8. 85.8 cm

Page 44

1. c
2. a
3. a

Page 45

1. 240
2. 450
3. 1,035
4. 240
5. 4,171
6. 1,155
7. 672
8. 87.5
9. 99.6
10. 484

Page 46

Part I

1. flew
2. swam
3. cried
4. drank
5. went
6. sped
7. ran
8. sang
9. drew
10. ate
11. bought
12. spoke
13. rode
14. wore
15. grew
16. froze
17. made
18. slept

Part II
Answers will vary but may include:

1. went
2. am
3. threw
4. groans
5. hid
6. are going
7. will live
8. earned

Page 47

Part I

1. 7 x 5 x 7 = 245 cubic units
2. 6 x 4 x 5 = 120 cubic units
3. 3 x 1 x 6 = 18 cubic units

Part II

1. 1^3 = 1 cubic unit
2. 7^3 = 343 cubic units
3. 5^3 = 125 cubic units

Page 48

Part I

1. premiere
2. despot
3. cavalcade
4. tribulation
5. toupee
6. bunker
7. testimony
8. correspondent

Part II

1. despot
2. bunker
3. premiere
4. toupee
5. tribulation
6. cavalcade
7. correspondent
8. testimony

Page 49

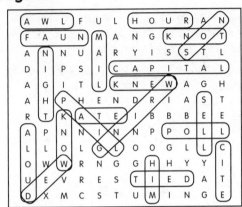

Page 50

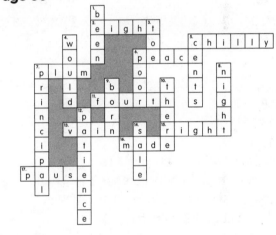

Page 51

1. b
2. b
3. d
4. c
5. d
6. a
7. c
8. d
9. c
10. b

Page 52

1. d
2. b
3. a
4. c

Page 53
Steal its chair.

Page 54

Part I

1. subject
2. subject
3. subject
4. verb
5. verb
6. verb
7. subject
8. verb

Part II
Answers will vary.

Answer Key *(cont.)*

Page 55
1. (11, 5)
2. (3, 0)
3. (6, 1)
4. (12, 12)
5. (4, 4)
6. (10, 8)
7. (8, 6)
8. (2, 11)
9. (6, 10)
10. (3, 7)
11. (1, 3)
12. (10, 2)

Page 56
1. According to the excerpt, the "green revolution" is mainly concerned with *how the production of a product will affect the environment.*
2. A "green consumer" is one who *considers many points before making a purchase.*
3. True
4. Answers will vary.

Page 57
1. 11/14
2. 1 13/18
3. 14/19
4. 82/87
5. 18/29
6. 1 1/4
7. 2/3
8. 5
9. 3/4
10. 3/4
11. 2 1/6
12. 3/7
13. 5/12
14. 8/9
15. 1 5/27
16. 3/10
17. 3 1/9
18. 6 1/4
19. 9 3/4
20. 1/4
21. 25/133
22. 5/64
23. 2 31/32
24. 33 3/4

Page 58
Answers will vary.

Page 59
Matt lives in apartment number 212.
Brandon lives in apartment number 213.
Gary lives in apartment number 210.
Louisa lives in apartment number 214.
Maria lives in apartment number 215.
Violet lives in apartment number 211.

Page 60
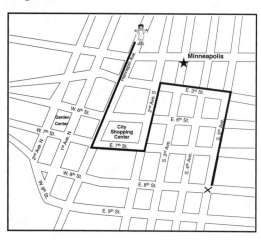

Page 61
1. c
2. b
3. d
4. d
5. c
6. a
7. a
8. c

Page 62
Answers will vary.

Page 63
1. 7/12 lb.
2. 1 5/12 lb.
3. 1/8 lb.
4. 1/12 lb.
5. 5 lbs.
6. 1/4 ft.
7. 1 7/10 lb.
8. 11/24 ft.
9. 6 cups
10. 1 19/30 lb.

Page 64
1. c
2. b
3. d

Page 65
Part I
1. $42.29
2. $196.08
3. $1,372.70

Part II
1. 1/10, .10, 10%
2. 1/4, .25, 25%
3. 9/20, .45, 45%
4. 3/20, .15, 15%
5. 4/5, .80, 80%
6. 7/8, .875, 87.5%
7. 77/100, .77, 77%
8. 1/20, .05, 5%
9. 11/50, .22, 22%
10. 2/5, .40, 40%

Page 66
Answers will vary, but check for appropriate punctuation and conjunctions.

Page 67
1. True
2. False
3. False
4. True
5. True
6. False
7. False
8. True

Page 68
Part I
My favorite poem, "Love Is Alive," was written by American poet Sophie Harrington. I read anything written by or about her that I can find. I was especially happy to find that, in my subscription to *Grandeur,* there was an article entitled "Up and Coming Poets" that featured Sophie and her work. As I read the article, I was surprised to discover that she has also written several short stories. Her latest short story, "The How and Why of It All," is scheduled to be in the next issue of *Grandeur.* Since I too am a writer, she has inspired me to begin writing a song that I've tentatively titled, "My Inspiration." I may even send her a copy of it, once I have it completed. Hopefully she will reply, but if she doesn't, she is still my favorite writer.

Answer Key *(cont.)*

Page 68 *(cont.)*

Part II

1. *The Sound of Music*—musical
2. *Titanic*—ship
3. *Hatchet*—book
4. *The Simpsons*—TV show

Sentences will vary.

Page 69

Galileo

Page 70

foreign language

horsing around

I see you are too wise for me.

paradise

checkup

domino

sitting on top of the world

one in a million

Go for it.

Page 71

1. 1999 and 2001
2. no
3. 88%
4. more; 21%
5. the percentage of 10–17 year olds who had an e-mail address in 2001
6. 4%
7. Answers will vary.
8. Answers will vary.

Page 72

1. c   3. b   5. b   7. c
2. a   4. a   6. c   8. a

Page 73

1. 55
2. 34
3. 4
4. 15
5. 4
6. New York
7. 256
8. 282
9. There are more electoral votes in California.
10. 14

Page 74

Part I

1. at the South Pole
2. during the speech
3. in the pan
4. on TV
5. under the table
6. to the movies
7. across the road
8. to the top

Part II

Answers will vary.

Page 75

Part I

1. 37   2. 38.5

Part II

1. 20   2. 300   3. 100 and 80

Page 76

1. c   2. c   3. b

4. Michael and Cheryl did not get along very well. They both did things to upset the other.
5. Answers will vary.
6. The word "smirk" means to smile *meanly*.

Page 77

1. Soccer (outdoor)
2. 19.6%
3. Netball
4. 18.2%
5. yes (2,500)
6. yes (6,400)
7. Other Athletics
8. the total number of boys and girls who played Australian-Rules Football

Page 78

Answers will vary.

Page 79

	5:45	6:00	6:15	6:30	6:45	Dessert	Rolls	Salad	Sodas	Spaghetti
Betty	X	X	O	X	X	X	X	X	X	O
Charice	X	O	X	X	X	X	O	X	X	X
Heidi	X	X	X	O	X	X	X	O	X	X
Paul	O	X	X	X	X	O	X	X	X	X
Roland	X	X	X	X	O	X	X	X	O	X

1. Betty arrived at ____6:15____ and brought the ____spaghetti____
2. Charice arrived at ____6:00____ and brought the ____rolls____
3. Heidi arrived at ____6:30____ and brought the ____salad____
4. Paul arrived at ____5:45____ and brought the ____dessert____
5. Roland arrived at ____6:45____ and brought the ____sodas____

Answer Key *(cont.)*

Page 80

Answers will vary.

Page 81

1. 528 in.	9	59 (58.67) in.
2. 911	11	83 (82.82)
3. 1,160 lbs.	13	89 (89.23) lbs.
4. 138 boxes	10	14 (13.8) boxes
5. 175 hours	13	13 (13.46) hours
6. $109	16	$7 ($6.81)

Page 82

1. Zeus asked Echo to distract his wife, Hera, by talking to her.

2. Zeus asked Echo to do this so that Hera wouldn't notice that he was flirting with other women.

3. Hera figured out what Zeus and Echo were up to and became furious. She took away Echo's ability to speak normally; Echo could only repeat the last word spoken to her.

4. Echo fell in love with Narcissus because he was so handsome.

5. Narcissus rejected Echo.

6. Nemesis punished Narcissus by making him fall in love with his own reflection.

7. Echo hid in a cave and wasted away until all that remained of her was her ability to repeat the last word spoken to her.

8. Unable to move away from his beautiful reflection, Narcissus wasted away at the edge of the pool until he vanished. A yellow flower grew in the place where he had sat.

Page 83

2. 4:5 or 4/5
3. 2:5 or 2/5
4. 5:2 or 5/2
5. 3:5 or 3/5
6. 5:3 or 5/3
7. 4:3 or 4/3
8. 3:4 or 3/4
9. 2:3 or 2/3
10. 3:2 or 3/2
11. 7:5 or 7/5
12. 5:7 or 5/7
13. 3:7 or 3/7
14. 7:3 or 7/3

Page 84

1. b   2. a   3. c   4. a   5. c

Page 85

1. 60
2. 50
3. 30
4. 60
5. 50
6. 55
7. 51
8. 40
9. 40
10. 80

Page 86

Answers will vary.

Page 87

2. 5   3. 8   4. 2.5   5. 12.41   6. 6

Page 88

1. b   2. b   3. c   4. d

Page 89

Answers will vary but may include:

					T	F	
				W	H	R	
				E	U	I	
				D	R	D	
				N	S	A	
S			T	U	E	S	D	A	Y
U					S	A	
N		M	O	N	D	A	Y
D					A		
S	A	T	U	R	D	A	Y
Y							

Page 90